THROUGH HELL TO
DUNKIRK

THROUGH HELL TO
DUNKIRK

A FRONTLINE STORY OF THE MIRACULOUS EVACUATION OF FRANCE IN WORLD WAR II

HENRY DE LA FALAISE

STACKPOLE
BOOKS

Essex, Connecticut
Blue Ridge Summit, Pennsylvania

STACKPOLE BOOKS
An imprint of The Globe Pequot Publishing Group, Inc.
64 South Main Street
Essex, CT 06426
www.globepequot.com

Distributed by NATIONAL BOOK NETWORK

Copyright © 1943 by The Military Service Publishing Company, Harrisburg, PA
Parts of this book appeared serially in *The Field Artillery Journal*, Washington, D.C.
First Stackpole edition 2024

British Library Cataloguing in Publication Information Available

Library of Congress Cataloging-in-Publication Data Available

ISBN 9780811776608 (paperback) | ISBN 9780811777087 (epub)

♾™ The paper used in this publication meets the minimum requirements of
American National Standard for Information Sciences—Permanence of Paper for
Printed Library Materials, ANSI/NISO Z39.48-1992.

To Major General Herbert L. Lumsden, D. S. O.,
M. C.; to Andrew, Bruce and Tim, and especially
to the memory of my friends, officers and men of
A Squadron, 12th Royal Lancers, who gave their
lives in Flanders that we may live on.

HENRY DE LA FALAISE.

12TH ROYAL LANCERS

Raised in 1697, this regiment in 1768 became known as the Prince of Wales' Light Dragoons. The Dragoons in 1816 were converted into Lancers and still bear the secondary title, "Prince of Wales'." Like the 9th, they served for the best part of a century in Ireland. Field Marshal Lord Birdwood is their Colonel.

Honours of The 12th Royal Lancers (Prince of Wales' Own)

Peninsula. Waterloo. South Africa, 1851-2-3. Sevastopol. Central India. Relief of Kimberley. France and Flanders, 1914-18.

Salute to Those Who Went
With Me

I

*D*URING *the latter part of January, 1940, I was attached
by the Headquarters of the Franco-British Military Mission of Liaison in Arras to the 12th Royal Lancers. I was
glad to have the assignment. It had interesting possibilities. As
a matter of fact, I was more than a bit proud to have been chosen
for it. This mechanized cavalry regiment, the only one of its
kind in the British Expeditionary Force, was indeed a superlatively
special unit. It was intended to be the reconnoitering eyes of
the B.E.F.'s High Command. With the additional mission to
make speedy contact with and fight the enemy far in advance of
all the other British troops, even the light tanks of the Divisional
Cavalry regiments.*

*For this purpose it had been equipped with armored cars.
Unfortunately, this car was obsolete. Certainly it was not com-
parable either to the French Panhard of 1939 or the German six-
wheeled Panzerkraftwagen. It had an open turret, armor-plate
only one-third of an inch thick and four wheels equipped with
bullet-proof tires, with armament consisting of a Bren gun and a
Boys anti-tank rifle (caliber .55) on universal mountings.*

*Built by the Morris concern, it had been intended for desert
warfare and patrolling against dissident tribes; certainly not to
fight against modern anti-tank weapons. But it had its points.
It afforded good visibility. It was fast and its radio telephone
communication system was excellent.*

1

II

I was immediately impressed by the magnificent bearing of the men who formed the regiment; tall, strong, bold-looking soldiers with weather-beaten faces. Old regulars, trained to a T, they could drill and snap to salute with a clockwork precision which is usually only to be found in that degree of perfection in the various Guards' battalions.

They were a group of fine, up-standing men, proud of their regiment's ancient traditions and battle honors; additionally proud that the regiment was known as "The Prince of Wales' Own." To mark this distinction, every N.C.O. wore three small silver feathers conspicuously on his arm above his insignia of rank.

The 12th Royal Lancers was one of those swanky cavalry outfits only to be found in pre-war England. It had not yet quite forgotten, much less forgiven, the fact that it had lost its horses and become mechanized. Imbued with the regiment's cavalry history, the men might be forgiven had they still tried to pretend that their horses were actually only just around the corner and that the order to mount and trot might come at any minute.

The officers all wore extremely well-cut riding breeches with bright canary-yellow buckskin strapping and highly-polished riding boots from the best London bootmakers. Their forage caps were of vivid scarlet, trimmed with gold, and turned out for them by a top-drawer London shop, at around four guineas apiece. Naturally, battle dress was worn on maneuvers or in billets in very bad weather.

As was befitting, the smartest of them all was the Lieutenant Colonel, L., who commanded the regiment.

Young, in his early forties, always in perfect physical trim, he embodied the spirit of the regiment. Extraordinarily intelligent, with an extremely penetrating mind, he was a superior type of officer. He had gone through staff college and served with distinction in the World War I. His gallantry in action had won him the Military Cross.

There was not a trooper, N.C.O., or officer in his regiment whom he did not know intimately and whose real worth he had not accurately rated. He saw through people and could quickly and accurately size them up. I never knew him to make a mistake about anyone. In military matters his foresight was near to being uncanny. In maneuvers he seldom was at fault in figuring what move the enemy was going to make. He had a faculty that seemed amazing for taking measures to counteract what they attempted or did and sometimes it struck us, even before the other fellow himself had figured his course. A strict disciplinarian, he was nonetheless eminently just; he invariably always saw the human side.

III

Four squadrons composed the regiment: a Headquarters Squadron and three forward Combat Squadrons each of which, in turn, consisted of a Headquarters Troop and three forward Troops. I was attached to "A" Squadron which was then billeted in a small windswept village of northern France. I had just had a trying two months in the far-flung outposts of the Saar sector, ten miles beyond the Maginot line, where I had lived and slept in shallow trenches in the Grossenwald, a few hundred yards from the German-held village of Waldwisse. The average winter temperature there was never much above zero, mostly under, so the change to a warm billet was more than welcome and my new quarters seemed sumptuous in comparison.

The other squadrons of the regiment were in different villages a few miles apart and we had little contact with them. Each was a definitely independent fighting unit and each was commanded by a Major. There was a French Liaison Officer attached to every squadron and also one at Regimental Headquarters with the Colonel, making a total of four of us in the regiment.

My squadron was commanded by a grand fellow, Major Andrew H. P., a tall, lanky, high-strung polo player of thirty-four, with a generous share of Irish blood. Fearless and enterprisingly bold, he was a born leader. Horses were his hobby; he was an expert on all kinds of racing and could, without omitting one, rattle off the names of the winners of the "Grand National" and the weights the horses carried. A real gambler at heart, you felt that he would stake on a toss of the martial dice, if challenged, his life and that of the officers and men of his squadron, without batting an eye. He was the kind who rides his mount ruthlessly and hard, without pity for man, including himself, or beast, in order to win a game—any game. Erratic, with a sometimes uncontrollable temper under provocation, he was either very kind or very stern with his command.

There was also another side to his character—a very charming side. I don't think the subalterns of his squadron ever found that; perhaps because he didn't intend them to. But I was privileged to have several glimpses of it, with the result that I became devoted to the man, and would have gladly yielded the ultimate sacrifice for him if need be.

His second-in-command was Major the Earl of E. He was not a regular officer and had recently come over from England. Attached to the regiment only temporarily, he would soon have to return to Northern Ireland to take command of a newly-formed armored-car regiment. His father had been killed in action in the last war. John, as he was known to us in the mess, was a keenly attractive-looking Irishman in his middle thirties. Gifted with enormous charm, he was a most likable character. Extremely quiet and calm, he kept his emotions in curb at all times, even under trying conditions. He was my conception of a thorough gentleman, of what an ideal gentleman should be. The fact that he bore one of the oldest titles of Ireland and England and was a peer of the realm apparently inclined him all the more strongly to be democratic and amiable to everyone. John's heart was in the right place. He always thought first of other people's feelings and of the welfare of the men of the squadron before his own. There was not a man in the whole outfit who would not have gone through hell and high water for his Lordship, the Earl.

The commanding officer of No. I Troop was Lieutenant Bruce S. Tall, fair-headed, blue-eyed, a little over twenty, he initially impressed persons who did not know him well as being dilettante, a wealthy dilettante. Though naturally indolent and insouciant, he could also, you felt, exhibit abundant courage, born of possession of real stamina if he deemed it worth the effort. He chose to cause one to believe that things military bored him inordinately. Perhaps they did. But it stood out that his troop was one of the best and that, on maneuver, he was the ablest of them all. I had supreme faith in Bruce, for I was confident that in a pinch he would never lose his head. He could be depended upon to do the right thing, even if it might be his pose to enact a hero's role with a slightly bored smile.

IV

Troop No. II was commanded by Second Lieutenant Peter A. It would be difficult to imagine a more charming and lovable boy. Tall and comely above the average in a masculine way, he looked about eighteen although he was a little above twenty. Always smiling and happy he savored life and delighted in making his troopers happy. He was in charge of the squadron's sports and outdoor games. In his love of beauty and cleanliness, he started his men to growing flower gardens in front of their billets. This was imitated by the other troops, and the little village in which we were billeted rapidly turned into a spring flower show. He also displayed eager ingenuity as a soldier and usually could be counted upon to spring a totally unexpected surprise during maneuvers on those who represented the enemy.

I was in command of a foot patrol one night, my object being to try to capture his armored car which was guarding a railroad crossing, or at least to put it out of action. It was pitch-dark. After crawling on my stomach over water-soaked ploughed fields

with my patrol, we finally surrounded his car. I was about to
give the signal to leap to the attack when hundreds of flashes
and a terrific noise like the cracking of a hundred rifles burst upon
us. He had secretly bought packets of Chinese fire-crackers
and laid them all over the ground surrounding his position, linked
them all together and touched them off from his car when he
heard us nearby. It may not have been according to the military
Hoyle of night maneuvers, but it made us laugh and proved that
we hadn't fooled him for one minute. I have described this
trifling episode only because I think it provides an excellent notion
of his character and his manner of doing things. To him, war
was a game and he was determined to enjoy it, to get as much
fun from it as he could, like the good sport he was.

Second Lieutenant, young Andrew R., also was a recent arrival
from England and commanded temporarily Troop No. III. Only
twenty-one, not tall, with fair hair and light blue eyes, he was
intelligent beyond the average, with a real sense of humor and
sharp wit which amused us all. He would have us believe that
his prime ambition was to sit in front of a fire, housed on his
landed estate, reading the Farmers' Gazette, or, with the help of
a glass of port of approved vintage doze over the staid columns of
The Times in a deep chair in his old-fashioned and ultra-ex-
clusive club in London. He was a graduate of an agricultural
school. Farming was his hobby and he would give us to understand that the price of hogs was of much more vital interest to
him than soldiering in the mucky fields of northern France. But
the truth was that he was really eager to be a crack officer and
was rapidly learning his trade, and doing it with a twinkle in his
eye and in a manner which, combined with his other agreeable
attributes, made him a high favorite in the squadron. He was
a brave, lovable lad.

We also had with us Second Lieutenant Tim B. who like most
of the others was tall and comely with brown, curly hair. He
never spoke much; he was a good soldier. By nature he was

cynical and showed sparse enthusiasm for maneuvers or the maintenance duties which fell to him. But one couldn't help feeling that he would display first class form in an emergency.

Our transport echelon was commanded by Second Lieutenant Basil. He was not a regular career officer. A lawyer by profession, he had recently joined us. Very intelligent and well-read, he always displayed eagerness to help others and was notably precise in his duties. He was a type quite apart from the other officers—a sturdy reliable John Bull.

V

With such a fine group of men as associates, life was more than agreeable and the weeks went by swiftly, filled with our daily routine. My duties were easy. They mostly consisted of smoothing out the inevitable frictions which arise between soldier and civilian, especially when the civilian is avaricious, as French peasants are apt to be, and the soldier is carefree, has plenty of money and is inclined to be lavish with it. There were always the same complaints: Our armored cars were forever backing into the same wall or damaging the same wooden post which we paid for over and over again, although they were never repaired. Then, when the spring thawing set in, there was the tearing up of the farmyards under the weight of our heavy armored cars and trucks.

Some of our men would be accused of filching straw for their bedding. We in turn would complain of café-owners who served beer after curfew. There were also in this village a few young ladies who needed watching, but all in all we were a happy family, and everyone from the Mayor down adored Les Lanciers. We had movies once a week in the parish hall. Sometimes officers and men would go up to Arras to attend musical shows brought over from England for the entertainment of the troops. Our Colonel saw to it that the squadrons were kept on their toes and that the men and the machines were superbly fit and ready for immediate action when the moment came. We knew that moment was sure to come and every one of us knew the role we were to play in it. We rehearsed it on maps, with sandboxes and on the terrain where we fought sham battles with the light tanks of the Divisional Cavalry regiments billeted in our neighborhood.

Most of these maneuvers would take us across the valley of the Ancre, which was supposed to represent the Dyle river, and past the huge war memorials at Thiepval and at Beaumont, the sanguinary battlefields of yesterday on which we were rehearsing the battle of tomorrow. We knew that we would have the French cavalrymen of the light mechanized divisions, known as D.L.M.'s, as comrades in the coming fight. They came to visit us, bringing their Panhards along so as to familiarize our men with the silhouette of the French armored car.

The Panhard was really a tank on wheels with an armor-plate of 12-mm to 16-mm and armed with one light machine gun and one 25-mm antitank gun. This excellent gun had a muzzle velocity of 3000 feet per second and could shoot either high-explosive or armor-piercing shells which had a penetration of 40-mm (1.6 inch) at 400 yards and 60-mm (2.4 inch) at 100 yards. It carried a crew of four. Slower than ours, it had a maximum speed of 45-50 m.p.h. Other regiments belonging to these divisions were equipped with Hotchkiss 35 and Somua 39 medium tanks. These powerful 20-ton machines had very thick armor and the best French antitank gun, the 47-mm. The D.L.M.'s—at the time there were only three in the French Army—were crack, hard-hitting units especially trained for their mission.

VI

The cold and snow that spring lasted until late, slowing down our training. On April 11th, two days after the Germans took Denmark and invaded Norway, an alert sent us flying north to the Belgian border to toe the mark at our jumping-off position.

My British comrades were rather puzzled at the Belgians' attitude. Their defenses were aimed as much against us as against their threatening eastern neighbors. Large antitank ditches and barbed-wire entanglements, road blocks made of cement, and other obstacles had been built across the roads we were to take in case they were invaded. Of course we hoped that they would pull them out of the way when the hour struck, but we knew that it would take them a certain length of time even then, and in war, as in love, every minute lost is really lost.

I had taken along with me a small camera. This was strictly against orders in the French Army. One afternoon, as I was snapping pictures of a group of us and also of some officers of the Guards battalion which were billeted in the same village with us, a French gendarme pounced on me and my camera, intent on arresting me. Had it not been for the prompt intervention of our friend Lord Cambridge, a Major in that Guards battalion and a member of the royal family, who jumped in a car and personally went to the gendarmerie headquarters to plead for me, my camera would have been confiscated and I would have been placed in a very awkward position. As it was, I lost only a film— and several bottles of champagne as forfeit to the mess.

We stayed on the border nearly two weeks in a state of constant alert—on a ten minutes' notice—then, just as suddenly as we had been ordered north, the emergency subsided and we returned to our little village near the Ancre valley.

On May 7th my long awaited furlough arrived and, after making my Major promise that he would send me a telegram if there was a new alert, I left the muddy village, not altogether unwillingly, headed for Paris.

H. de la F.

FIRST DAY

Friday, May 10th, Paris, 5 hrs.

THE HOWLING SIRENS of the air raid alarm bring me out of bed. The booming of gunfire shakes the clear spring dawn. Running to the open window, I see three large German bombers cruising leisurely at about 6000 feet over southwestern Paris. The antiaircraft batteries are vainly trying to get their range, but their shells seem to burst harmlessly behind the bombers. No fighter aircraft rise to challenge them. There is a strange and peculiar feeling in the morning atmosphere which makes me uncomfortable. These enemy raiders are not dropping bombs; they are just hovering over Paris, slowly, menacingly taking their time, like vultures waiting for a vicarious kill—that they may gorge.

I cannot go back to sleep. I turn on the radio at 7 a.m. and hear the agitated commentator broadcast the most important news he has had to deliver since war was declared last September: At daybreak the German armies have hurled their might against the Belgian and French defenses in a mass frontal attack. Most of the Allied airfields have been raided simultaneously by thousands of planes. Countless numbers of our aircraft have been destroyed on the ground and in their hangars!

The long awaited blow has been struck at last, but it has been struck by the enemy.

Goodbye leave! I must rejoin my regiment at once. Twelve hours later I am at the Gare du Nord, fighting my way with my

11

friend Bob through a milling crowd of officers and men on leave, starting to rejoin their units. The huge waiting room is filled with hundreds and hundreds of civilans, Belgians, Dutchmen, and others, trying to return to their countries to answer the call of mobilization issued this morning by their governments.

The trains are overcrowded. Men pile into them with their equipment as best they can. It is like fighting your way into the New York subway at a rush hour. Bob and I use subway methods and we finally succeed in squeezing into an already full compartment in the fast train leaving for Lille.

Bob is the French Liaison Officer of a squadron of the 4/7th Dragoons, B.E.F. The last time I had seen him was on a cold gray morning four months ago when he relieved me on the outpost line in the Hartbusch sector, where I had spent all of December and part of January, crawling through the frozen woods making liaison between the British and the French outpost platoons, sometimes under disturbingly accurate enemy fire from machine guns, trench mortars, or 105 howitzers. This period may have seemed like a "phoney" war to some who were sitting in warmer and less dangerous quarters, but not as far as we were concerned. We saw around us too many men wounded and killed to think there was anything "phoney" about the German artillery and machine-gun fire.

At 7 p. m. our train stops suddenly just outside the station at Albert in the Somme. We hear people running along the tracks and shouting. The little town has just been bombed. As I look out of the car window, I see bloody stretchers being carried to a spot where lie the smoking ruins of a house, just beyond the station. Further up the main street a small building is in flames. After a few minutes the train pulls out and, as we pass the station, we see wounded men and women lying side by side on the ground in front of the *salle d'attente* which has been hastily transformed into a dressing station.

At Arras, I leave Bob, who is going on to Douai. I learn from a gendarme that Arras has had seven air attacks today. The narrow streets of the old town and the suburbs have been ma-

chine-gunned by low-flying Heinkels; the nearby flying fields have
been torn up by high-explosive bombs.

As I walk out on the Place de la Gare carrying my kit, the
alarm sirens scream again and the booming anti-aircraft guns
pepper the sky overhead with black puffs. Everyone scurries for
shelter. I run on through the deserted streets towards the house
where I know I shall find the headquarters of the French liaison
group attached to this British G.H.Q.

Captain is sitting in the small office. He soon gives me the
latest news which has come in to him. He has heard that the
regiment to which I am attached, the 12th Royal Lancers, passed
through Brussels this afternoon and was wildly cheered by the
population of the Belgian capital.

Later reports place the Lancers' armored squadron as speeding
eastward to meet the oncoming enemy. He tells me to wait for
our C.O., who is off on a mission for the British High Command,
as he alone can give me my definite orders. I do not have long
to wait. He arrives at 21.00 hrs. and takes me with him to the
British G.H.Q. to get complete information as to the exact whereabouts of my regiment.

Through pitch black, narrow, winding streets, and after being
challenged by half a dozen grim-looking British sentries, we reach
a small door leading to the deep crypts under the huge eighteenth
century Archibishop's Palace. There the brains of the B.E.F's
General Staff are feverishly at work. Large maps, hung on the
walls, show accurately the locations of the advancing British units.
As new reports come in, these positions are changed and moved
forward. The scene reminds me of one I saw in a crowded New
York stockbrokers' office during the 1929 crash—the maps repre-
senting the big board and the regiments the various stocks.

I stand for awhile in a corner watching this tremendously interesting scene. The Cdt. goes to talk to some of the officers.
After a few minutes he calls me over to a table where a young
staff captain tells me that the latest reports indicate that the
Lancers, which, with the rest of the mechanized cavalry, form the
advance guard, are heading for Tirlemont, east of Louvain and
the strategic river Dyle.

From what I hear around me, I gather that the general impression seems to be that the German units which have crossed the Belgian border north of Liege are pushing northwestward toward the south of Holland, rather than heading straight on to the Dyle. According to the pre-arranged plan, the British infantry will reach the Dyle river position tomorrow and will dig in behind it. The French will be doing the same on the right of the B.E.F. between Wavre and Namur and behind the Meuse river between that city and Sedan.

23.00 hrs. I have obtained a small room in an old-fashioned hotel on the famous "Place du Beffroi" and eaten a sandwich before lying down on the hard bed in the candle-lit room to try to sleep. There have been two more air raids since my arrival in Arras and the guns practically haven't let up for a minute. Tomorrow morning I am leaving for Belgium.

Saturday, May 11th

I LEAVE ARRAS at 8.00 hrs. with the Cdt. by car. He is taking me only as far as Tournai, in Belgium, about ten miles from the French border, after which I shall be on my own. We reach the lovely town at 10 o'clock and halt on the main square near the fine old cathedral with its seven spires. Our car is immediately surrounded by cheering citizens. They gape at us as if we were the advance guard of an incoming circus.

After wishing me good luck, the Commandant leaves me and I set out to change some francs into belgas. This is not easy. The banks are closed and I have to pay an exorbitant rate for my belgas. I also buy some very detailed maps of the country east and west of Brussels; then I walk to the railway station at the other end of town and am lucky enough to find a fast train leaving immediately for the Belgian capital.

At 14.00 hours I am in Brussels. It has been bombed twice early this morning and the streets are crowded with excited soldiers and civilians. I manage finally to find a taxi which is willing to take me to the French Embassy, miles away from the station. I had been advised by the Cdt. to report there as he thought that the Military Attaché or someone in his office would certainly find some way to help me reach my regiment.

When I get there, I waste thirty minutes in an office where, in the absence of the Military Attaché, no one seems to know anything. The sight of a Frenchman in uniform and full war kit trying to locate a British armored-car regiment seems to fill every-one with surprise and suspicion. As I stand there waiting to speak to someone in authority, I hear a suggestion that I be sent to a camp of concentration for officers and men who have lost their units. I tell them that I have a taxi waiting outside and that I wish to be allowed to go out to pay the driver.

I walk out of the Embassy, jump in my taxi and tell the man to drive off at full speed towards the British Military Attaché's office at the other end of the town. We are halted several times by helmeted soldiers as we pass by the King's palace where all traffic is stopped. But when they see my uniform, they wave us on. We reach the British Embassy in record time.

There, I find a very charming Brigadier standing in the street in front of the building. He, too, is trying to rejoin his brigade and is waiting for news, but he tells me that he has good reason to believe that the Lancers are, as I expected, on the immediate left of the French Armored Cavalry Divisions, the third "Division Legere Mecanique," which is operating on the left flank of the French Army somewhere around and south of St. Tround. They have already engaged the enemy.

So I get back into my faithful taxi and drive to the railway station only to find that the train service towards the east has been stopped.

As I sit in the buffet wondering what my next move should be, an elderly and prosperous-looking gentleman comes up to my table and insists on paying for my glass of beer. I am the first French soldier he has seen since the last war and he introduces me to several friends who are sitting with him. I learn from them that he is the burgomaster of the town of Wavre, the very town I am trying to reach. And best of all that he is driving home in his car and will be only too glad to take me along with him.

We drive through the beautifully-kept Foret de Soingnes, of which the inhabitants of Brussels are so proud, and reach the small town of Wavre and the burgomaster's house at 16.30 hrs. I am introduced to the whole family and compelled to sit and visit with them while he runs down to the cellar to fetch a bottle of his best wine in which he wants to drink to my health before I leave for the battle front.

When he returns with his precious cargo, we proceed to the dining room where his agreeable and plump wife sits at the head of the table and watches us smilingly as we ceremoniously drink to France, to Belgium, to Holland, to England. I am grateful that there are no other Allies to be toasted; had there been I probably never would have reached my squadron.

Finally I take leave of my hosts and the peaceful atmosphere of their comfortable home and find myself standing at the corner of a road leading over the Dyle towards the east.

During our various maneuvers and sandbox exercises of the preceding months, we had often rehearsed our advance east of the Dyle, and I remember that the Major and I had jokingly decided that a certain chateau a mile or so east of Gray-Doiceau would make an ideal spot for our squadron headquarters, as the map showed that it was situated in the middle of a wooded park. So I decide that it would not be a bad idea to try and get there and find out if our plans had been followed.

Wandering down the road, I see in the distance some soldiers of a Scottish battalion of the 2d Division which have apparently just arrived. I join them and introduce myself to a young officer. He tells me that he has been searching vainly for a decent spot in which to establish his men's cook house, but since he speaks no French, he is in deep water. I, too, tell him my problems and we make a bargain: if I find a suitable place for the cook house, he will let me have a small lorry and a driver who will take me ten miles across the river, but no farther. This is sporting of him, since it might get him into trouble as the territory east of the Dyle is out of bounds for his battalion. I immediately get busy and within fifteen minutes the company's cook is settled and happy, and the Scotsman orders the lorry driver to take me ten miles east and to return at once.

We drive for five miles on an excellent road through the lovely green valley of the Dyle and soon reach the first houses of Gray-Doiceau. I see no sign of British troops there, and we continue on toward Bausart and climb the hill leading to the high ground on which runs the Louvain-Namur highway.

As we pass by a large farm, I see the insignia of the regimental headquarters of the British 4/7 Dragoons on the front gate, so I jump out of the lorry and tell my driver to return to Wavre and convey my thanks to his officer. Just then, Lt. Mera, French liaison officer with that Dragoon regiment, walks out of the court-yard; I know then that I am on the right track.

Lt. Mera tells me he has heard that my unit is somewhere east of here, patrolling between Tirlemont and Jodoigne and that my best bet is to ride towards it in the trucks transporting the French motorized infantry of the 3d Mechanized Cavalry Division which are driving in the direction of the front. Shortly after, I see a long line of trucks coming up the hill. Their markings show that they belong to the 3d D.L.M.—they are carrying the 8th "Dragon portes." Lt. Mera and I stop the officers' command car and a few minutes later I am sitting in it driving towards Jodoigne.

These troops are going into the line to take up a position somewhere near Hannut. The forward armored reconnaissance units of their division have already made contact with the German spearheads. The officers and men alike seem to have magnificent morale; they are eager to come to grips with the enemy and are full of confidence in their excellent weapons and leadership. Their whole attitude is that they are going to give the Boche a kick in the face that he will remember and which will send him reeling back to his homeland. They are particularly proud of the new Somua tanks with which their division is equipped, and its wonderful 47 mm. antitank gun which they say will punch the German panzers so full of holes that they will look like sieves by the time they get through with them.

They also ply me with questions about the British army and I tell them that they have nothing to worry about as far as the fighting qualities of their Allies are concerned.

As we drive eastward, getting ever closer to the front line, the booming of guns grows louder while every now and again explosions like claps of thunder ahead of us make us wonder whether the Germans are using exceptionally heavy artillery or dropping bombs, though we have seen no enemy planes so far.

At 18.30 hrs., only two miles from Jodoigne, I catch sight of a British armored car which is stopped under a clump of trees on the right side of the road. As we reach it and halt, a face appearing in the turret lights up with a broad grin as it sees me. Under the dirt and stubble of beard which covers it, I hardly recognize my usually spick-and-span friend, Bruce, Commander of No. I Troop of my squadron.

My quest is ended.

I take leave of the *Dragons* and hurry to the armored car, congratulating myself on the luck which has brought me in less than 24 hours straight from the streets of Paris to my unit, hundreds of miles away, without a single error. I feel relaxed now that I have reached my objective.

Rapidly I am told about the day's events. This troop has just come back to this quiet spot to try and fix their wireless sets, damaged in a dive-bombing attack which they have just undergone in a village east of here. The men are still badly shaken from it.

As we talk, the third car of the troop drives up. It is Sgt. Ditton's car. It had been practically blown off the road by the bomb blast, but succeeded in righting itself and is now reporting. The wireless receiver set on this car also is out of order, but the radio operator thinks he can still transmit.

I have been assigned to Ditton's armored car and Bruce asks me to go forward and effect a liaison with the French armored brigade operating on our right flank.

We drive through Jodoigne, then take the Hannut road to Jauche where I see some French cavalrymen who direct me to Petit Orp, a tiny hamlet two miles north of Jandrain. There, in a small room at the back of an abandoned farmhouse I find the C. P. of the French brigade of Cuirassiers. After only a short wait, I am introduced to the Colonel who commands it. I give him our position and tell him that my squadron's mission is to keep in close contact with the left of his brigade, but that, on account of the rather fluid and rapidly changing positions of the armored car and motorcycle platoons composing his left wing, I should like his views on how we can best accomplish our mission.

Picking up a map, he shows me the point where his troops now are. I note them down on my map while he tells me that he

thinks the best thing for us to do for the moment is to keep watch
tonight south of the Tirlemont-St. Trond highway. His own
armored car units by then will be based on the Tirlemont-Hannut
highway between Goetsenhoven and Opheilissen.

There seems to be no doubt in the minds of the French staff
officers here that the Germans are trying to repeat exactly their
maneuver of 1914 in Belgium by pushing their light armored
forces, as they then did their cavalry, through the Hannut gap
and then marching north toward Tirlemont, Diest and Antwerp.
They all feel that tomorrow they will have to fight a hard and
perhaps decisive battle when the enemy, emerging from Hannut,
comes into contact with the D.L.M.'s main forces.

As I drive back to where I had left Bruce and think of all I
have just heard, I am reminded of the battles of August 1914
along the Gette River, the loss of Tirlemont, and the Belgian retreat to the line of the Dyle. All those names, which had meant
nothing to me at the time I first read them, are now staring at
me from the map which I am studying.

Night is beginning to fall when I reach No. I Troop and make
my report to Bruce who tries to communicate it to the Major by
wireless, hoping that he will receive it even though we can get
no answer. Our radio can still transmit, but not receive. The
three armored cars are now concealed in a small wood a mile
west of Jodoigne. The crews are making tea and we are having
a light supper of biscuit and bully beef when a dispatch rider
from Squadron Headquarters brings orders to move north of
Hoegarden, three miles south of Tirlemont. This means that
our message has been received.

Bruce sends me ahead in the armored car with Sgt. Ditton so
that I may speak up in French if we are challenged by French
or Belgian troops unfamiliar with the silhouette of a British armored
car, which, by the way, bears no identifying marks except a white
square on both sides of the rim of the turret and a small British
flag which we are to pull out and wave in time of need. This
would hardly be satisfactory at night.

As we reached Jodoigne, we find that the road is so filled with
refugees that we can hardly move forward. We waste valuable

time trying to cut through their column to make a left turn on the
Tirlemont road. As we pass the last houses of the village and
reach the top of the small hill, the drone of the engines of several
enemy bombers fills the night air above us and the sky to the
east is red with the glare rising from flaming villages.

Slowly, carefully, we move on through the flow of fleeing
humanity: old men pushing small carts filled with their families'
hastily-gathered belongings; women wrapped in shawls and loaded
with bundles, dragging children of all ages behind them; tired,
wild-eyed children; others are urging goats and cows before them.
Every now and again they start to run. I can hear frantic screams
when bombs plaster the road ahead. We have to stop while this
flowing human tide brushes by us, bumping into the armored
car as it stumbles along, accompanied by the crash of nearby explosions and the bleating and mooing of the terrified farm beasts.

We have been on our way now for nearly an hour and have
covered only about eight miles when we pass through the village
of Lumay and are free of the refugee column.

At 22.45 hrs. we reach our destination and halt the armored
car alongside of a small villa a mile east of the deserted village
of Hoegarden. On the other side of the road stretch out the iron-
fenced walls of a large factory. The car is facing west toward
the railroad tracks and the river, which run half a mile away.
Bruce's car is concealed somewhere back of them, in the village
proper. Our Bren and Boys guns are trained eastward, covering
the crossroad to Outgarden, fifty yards away.

There is a strange silence around me. Not a real silence, since
I can hear in the distance the crackling of burning timber and
can see smoke and flames rise over the horizon under the starlit
sky; yet the silence exists. It is due to the complete absence of
human sounds. I can "hear" that the houses are empty around
me, that there are no cattle breathing heavily in the stables, that
no life is left in this village, where not even a dog barks.

24.00 hrs. Exhausted, Sgt. Ditton, who has been on his feet
for forty-eight hours, is lost to the world. He is fast asleep, all
crumpled up in a heap at the bottom of the car and wedged somehow between all the paraphernalia which clutters it, his head on

an ammunition case. Every time I move, I have to be careful not to kick him in the face as I stand up in the turret keeping watch.

The fires ahead die down, but parachute flares are dropping now all over the countryside, lighting up the horizon with blue-white halos in the direction of the St. Trond road. On my left, and in the distance, comes the intermittent muffled rattle of machine-gun fire and frequent loud explosions which seem to proceed from Tirlemont shake the windows of the houses around me and make me grip tighter the butts of the guns at my elbows. They are both fully loaded and ready for immediate action.

THIRD DAY

I AM BEGINNING to feel chilly and sleepy; my feet are numb from standing so long in this turret. To my relief, I feel Sgt. Ditton stirring. His head pops up at my side. He is feeling much better for his two hours' nap. I jump out of the car and walk to the railroad tracks where I find one of our dispatch riders on duty, straddling his motor cycle. Crossing the tracks, I reach a small bridge. A signpost near it indicates the name of the river. It is the Gette. I slide down the steep embankment and splash some water over my head and face, but though the water is icy cold, it does not succeeed in making me feel less sleepy. So I return to the armored car and curl up in the bottom of it in much the same position assumed by Sgt. Ditton before me and promptly pass out.

3.00 hrs. The whine of the generator on our wireless set wakes me up. I have slept only thirty minutes and am cold and stiff, but a biscuit and a piece of chocolate make me feel somewhat warmer. Burns, the radio operator, who has spent part of the night fixing his wireless set, is calling the command car with a patience which is at last rewarded.

A message comes through from Squadron Headquarters. It is from the Major: he sends me his congratulations for finding and rejoining the squadron so speedily, and wants me to try to gain contact with the left flank of the French armored car unit of the 3rd D.L.M. Regimental Headquarters wants to know the exact positions held by the French Cuirassiers, as it is feared that the

Germans might be pushing on to Tirlemont after going through Hannut which they seem to have captured. I am to find out and report. Also I am to tell the Cuirassiers that the 4/7 Dragoons are on their way up to reinforce them and should be available at noon.

I send a dispatch rider to Bruce with this message. The man soon returns with another dispatch rider and a message that I am to go ahead, but to take both motorcyclists with me for safety.

It is still dark as we set off eastward in the armored car through the heavy morning mist. We pass through Outgarden and I decide to take a rather dubious country road leading to Goetsenhoven on the Tirlemont-Hannut highway in hope of reaching Opheilissen from there, that being the village that was mentioned at the French Cuirassiers H.Q. last night.

This road is so sandy and soft that our rear wheels skid into a deep rut and we get stuck. After some anxious moments, we finally pull out, thanks to the help of the extra D.R., and drive on.

We find Goetsenhoven deserted and almost completely destroyed. I send a D.R. to have a look around the crossroad in the center of the village. He returns shortly, reporting that he had seen a large armored car farther up in the village. He thinks it is a French one. We move on cautiously and, as we reach the church square, I see through the dim light an armored car speeding toward us. I wave the Union Jack while Ditton takes aim the Boys gun, in case—.

It is a Panhard! The turret opens as we pull up alongside and the head of a smiling Cuirassier sergeant appears. I ask him where I can find his squadron commander and he tells me that the C.P. is in a tumble-down farmhouse just outside the village on a small road leading to an airfield.

I immediately proceed there, but leave the armored car concealed under a shed in a farmyard a few hundred yards before reaching the C.P., riding the rest of the way on the back of the D.R.'s motor cycle.

After identifying myself, I am shown into a small room where a Major of the Cuirassiers is sitting at a small table studying a map by the light of a nearly burnt-out candle. As he turns around, I recognize Cdt. Halbessart with whom I had dined at our mess only a month ago.

This makes everything easy. No introductions are needed and he tells me of his pleasure at having met my Colonel and the officers of my squadron. Then we get down to business as I explain my mission.

He doesn't know much more than we do about the situation around Hannut. The two squadrons under his command have spent a quiet night relatively, watching the roads east of here on the high ground between the Tirlemont-St. Trond highway and Landen.

As we talk, a report comes in that two of his Panhard troops are being engaged by light enemy tanks in the neighborhood of Rumsdorp. They are holding their own. He is very optimistic about the situation as a whole, though he does think that the Germans have already gone through Hannut. As I study the map, I can't help realizing that if they have, some of their main tank forces should soon be rolling up the road which passes through this village. This is the only road from Hannut to Tirlemont, and Hannut is only about ten miles away.

He then shows me on his map—and I copy on mine—the points where German panzer units have been attacked by the Panhards of his group. Some of these the day before have gone as far as the outskirts of St. Trond.

As I am about to leave, the Cdt.'s *Ordonnance* brings us each a cup of hot coffee which tastes as hot coffee always does taste at such times. As we sip it, he tells me that theoretically some elements of a Belgian cavalry division should be holding the Tirlemont-St. Trond road. I decide to return to Hoegarden only after I have located the Belgian defenses, so as to be able to bring a more complete report as to who is holding what in this sector.

After taking leave of the Commandant, I find my dispatch rider, who is surrounded by Cuirassiers admiring his fine motorcycle and modern equipment. I return to the armored car and we move off towards the highway which we cross, taking a small road through the fields. This leads us through the small hamlet of Meer to Wukmersen. Both are badly damaged by yesterday's bombs and incendiaries and completely devoid of any sign of life.

It is now 4.30 hrs. The red glow of the rising sun lights up the sky to the east as squadron after squadron of large dark enemy bombers roar by over us at a height of not more than 1,000 feet. They don't pay any attention to us; they are going to plaster our main positions along the Dyle.

As we near the turn to a small country road leading to Haken-dover, a small village bordering the Tirlemont-St. Trond highway, we stumble onto a road block manned by some Belgian soldiers who tell me that they belong to the crack "Guides" regiment. I jump out of the armored car, show my credentials, and am led to a major who is in command.

His men are placing antitank guns behind some overturned carts and farming utensils; they seem rather tired and dirty. I learn that they have retreated from St. Trond, twelve miles away, during the night and have had very severe losses. The Belgian Major shows me on his map the positions which the cavalry corps to which he belongs are to take up on the west bank of the Gette River, north and east of Tirlemont. He adds that he thinks they will be able to hold them for awhile as they will have good artillery support. I then give him the information I have gathered from Cdt. Hal-bessart, and he seems delighted to know that his right flank is securely held by Franco-British cavalry.

We now swing our car around toward Hoegarden and speed back to it as fast as the state of the road permits.

5.30 hrs. We pull up alongside of Bruce's armored car in Hoe-garden. He has received orders for me to proceed at once to Squadron C.P. in Meldert, which is on top of the hill about a mile west, to report to the Major. Just as I am leaving, some Pan-hards pass by us, followed by Cdt. Halbessart. He tells me that the enemy is pushing up the Tirlemont-Hannut road and he has had to withdraw his C.P. which he will establish on the west side of Hoegarden.

I find our Squadron C.P. at the farthest end of Meldert close to the churchyard. The Major and his second-in-command are both sitting on the ground with their backs to the wall of a house near the forward link armored car which is concealed in a shed.

Forty-eight hours without sleep show clearly on their drawn faces and in their bloodshot eyes. But their greeting is warm and cheery as I sit down and give them all the information I have collected

so far. The Major immediately telephones this to Regimental Headquarters and, when he returns, he transmits to me the Colonel's
greetings and thanks. Just then Trooper Machin, his clever and
resourceful batman, appears with hot tea and boiled eggs which he
has mysteriously conjured up.

As there is nothing more for me to do for the moment, and,
realizing that this is Sunday and I should therefore look my best,
I decide that a wash and a shave might be a rightful occupation.
Machin, who agrees with me, soon brings forth a basin full of hot
water which I put to immediate use.

At 7.00 hrs. the roaring sound of German bombers makes us
look up. There are dozens of them in perfect flying formation,
apparently returning from the Dyle and the west. They sweep by
overhead and soon are replaced by others who first fly low over
Tirlemont to drop some bombs, then straight on to Hoegarden
which they literally deluge with bombs. We can follow them
plainly as they drop through the air. The bombers pass overhead
as they circle around, but they evidently don't see our well-concealed
vehicles as they ignore us, returning once more to drop more explosives on the hapless village which harbors the Cuirassiers and
our No. I Troop.

Smoke and flames are rising from the village below us, but Bruce
reports that all is well with his troop and that his guns, as well as
the heavier machine guns of the French, are blazing away at the
raiders. After awhile, either on account of this defense or because
they have no more bombs, the Heinkels climb out of range and
disappear to the northeast.

9.00 hrs. No. I Troop needs information and asks me to get in
contact again with Cdt. Halbessart. The Colonel phones in as
I am about to leave for Hoegarden. Headquarters are worried over
a report which has just reached them to the effect that German
tanks are swarming over the countryside between Hannut, Jodoigne,
and Tirlemont. I am to find out if this is true and, if so, ask the
Cuirassiers what line they intend to hold on to in case we should
be forced to retreat. I am also to tell them that the 4/7 Dragoons'
light tanks are being rushed up in support.

Another, but this time lighter, bombing attack delays my arrival in Hoegarden. The village is in ruins now; the road is strewn with wreckage and I have trouble locating the French C.P. At last I am directed to a bomb-shattered farmhouse where I find Cdt. Halbessart and the Colonel in command of the Cuirassier regiment standing in the only room which has a semblance of ceiling and walls left.

Reports of the fight which their brigade is waging keep coming in. The Panhards are doing well and fighting like mad. They have destroyed at least fifteen German tanks during the last hour. One of the troop commanders, Lt. de St. E., enters the room. As he stands smartly at attention, clicks his heels and salutes his Colonel, I notice that two German tommyguns are swung over his shoulder. In his right hand he holds a German helmet dripping with blood. He presents these trophies to his Colonel and reports that his *peloton* has destroyed five German light tanks near Opheilissen before the three Panhards under his command were knocked out of action. He begs the Colonel to be given another armored car immediately so that he and his troop may get back into the fight.

Cdt. Halbessart takes the brave young officer along to see what can be done and if the men are in a state to be sent back into the fight immediately.

The Colonel, whose expression shows his pride at the good showing of his men, asks me to share some of his sandwiches, while he shows me the latest positions of the enemy tanks on his map. It makes me very uneasy to see how near they are to us now. This leads me to ask what possible line his unit expects me to take in case of a withdrawal. But he refuses to envisage such a move now and asks me to convey this to my Colonel.

"We will fight on this line," he adds, "and die here if necessary, as we must absolutely gain time in order to enable the troops on the Dyle to build up a strong position."

"Nous ne reculerons pas, dites le à nos amis," are his parting words as we shake hands.

As I return to my car, I pass the first tanks of the 4/7 Dragoons which are entering a farmyard. I tell the officer in the leading tank where he will find the French Cavalry C.P. and advise him that it might be a good thing to report there at once. He says he will so soon as his French liaison officer arrives. Shortly afterwards,

Lt. M., the French Liaison Officer, rides up in a Bren gun carrier. I tell him the situation briefly and leave for Meldert.

I describe my visit and its results to the Major who communicates them at once to the Colonel.

The sun is very hot by now and we sit in the shade under a hedge watching swarms of German planes of every sort roaming at will all over the whole front.

After a little while our Colonel arrives in his command car. I repeat to him the message from the French, but he is worried that we might be turned from the south, so I get in his car with him and we return to the Cuirassiers where he has a talk with their C.O.

The French Colonel does not feel so sure of his ground now as the medium 20-ton Somuas, the pride of the D.L.M., have been thrown into the battle and have been severely knocked about. The Germans also have brought up heavier tanks, probably the 22-ton Pz-KwIV, which are armed with 75 mm. guns.

When I return to Meldert I see three British fighter planes go after the German Luftwaffe with lightning speed and with great courage, considering that they are outnumbered ten to one. They clear the sky as if by magic, but one of them gets into trouble east of Tirlemont and we see the pilot bail out of his flaming aircraft. Though he has apparently fallen in enemy territory, the Major sends one of our armored cars immediately to try to pick him up.

14.30 hrs. The French report that they have lost twenty Somuas and fifteen Panhards. One of our No. I Troop cars is damaged. No. II Troop has killed fifteen motorcycle scouts and destroyed a German armored car at point blank range. Our No. III Troop, which at one point was surrounded, managed to slip away unscathed. And the grateful R.A.F. flyer who has been rescued is having a sandwich and a glass of beer before being sent back to the rear. He is Squadron Leader Tomlinson and he and his pilots have shot down more than thirteen enemy planes in two days.

A report comes in that some German tanks have entered Tirlemont, but that the Belgian cavalry is still resisting. The French D.L.M.'s on our right are withdrawing slightly and our squadron has orders to move up to the east of Tirlemont to support the Belgians on the River Gette line.

15.30 hrs. The Major tells me to go ahead in the first armored car. His follows me at three hundred yards with the D.R.'s between us. We are moving along at a good speed when all of a sudden we are greeted by several bursts from a machine gun hidden behind a road block just outside the village of Upvelp. Bullets spatter against the car. I tell the driver to speed on toward the flashes and I wave the Union Jack above my head as it does not seem possible that the enemy could have already reached this spot at our rear.

When we get within two hundred yards of the machine guns, the firing stops, and I see several British soldiers with rifles run out of a farmyard. I yell to them who we are and they yell back apologies. They belong to a Divisional Cavalry Light Tank Hussar Regiment, and it was difficult for them to recognize us on account of the dust raised by my armored car and the motorcyclists, and the position of the sun.

Seeing no signs of the Major back of me, I send a D.R. in his direction with a message that all is well and that I intend to continue ahead. As I wait for the motorcyclist to return, I study my map and realize that I have gone too far west and past the small country lane leading to Kumtich which is the point where I intended to join the Tirlemont-Louvain highway. My D.R. returns while the armored car is backing up and turning around and says that the Major has already gone ahead to Kumtich. I am to follow him there.

We reach the highway without incident and there I find the Major's D.R. waiting for me with a message to proceed to St. Martins as the C.O. has decided to go right into Tirlemont to find out if it is true about German tanks being already in the city.

17.30 hrs. No. II Troop passes by in a cloud of dust with Peter shouting to me that they are off to hold a small bridge on the River Gette, north of Tirlemont. Bruce and his troop speed by shortly after, followed by young Andrew and his armored cars. They all disappear down the road to Bunsbeek, enveloped by dust.

The Major returns from Tirlemont. He has driven through the streets and says that he has seen no trace of the enemy. He has found the little town badly damaged by the bombing, the streets full of debris of all kinds and no living souls excepting some Belgian troops near the road to St. Trond.

We establish the squadron C.P. at St. Martins in the courtyard of a small inn. The artillery of the Belgian cavalry division is placed on the hills just outside and east of the village. It consists of four batteries of French long 75's. The sixteen guns are in well-camouflaged pits, their positions stretching for nearly a mile. They fire continually to harass the enemy on the road to St. Trond. Two German Henschel observation planes are hovering above trying to locate them. If they do, things might get pretty hot for us and for the small inn, which is not thirty feet from the crossroad.

As my French military training has always taught me to avoid crossroads like poison, I feel obliged to warn the Major. But he just grins at me and tells me to hop in the staff car with him as he intends to reconnoiter our front lines.

19.00 hrs. We are on our way toward the small road which runs parallel to the Gette northeast of Tirlemont. We stop first at Oplinter and examine Lt. Andrew's position guarding a small destroyed bridge across the river. Then we go to Drieslinter where we find Peter guarding another blown-up bridge. Two miles farther on we see two cars of the No. III Troop and Bruce. He looks very tired. Sporadic machine-gun fire is coming from the small woods just across the River. The last car of Bruce's troop is in position half a mile farther on near the end of the village of Budingen.

We drive on to examine it, but, when we get to the first houses of the village where the road turns toward the bridge we stumble on a Belgian outpost line held by half a company and at least one antitank gun. They are firing like mad with rifles, machine guns, and the antitank gun which is placed at the cross-roads at the entrance of the village. We can't see what they are firing at, but we are placed between their fire and the enemy. The Major and I both grab rifles and jump out of the car which turns around at full speed to get to a place of concealment behind a house two hundred yards farther back. We crawl on the paved road toward the middle of the village and the place where we should normally find our third armored car.

The Belgians are waving at us to get out of the way. The bullets from their rifles and machine guns are making annoying sounds

over our heads. They seem very excited, but Andrew is as calm as
if he were merely crossing the traffic at Piccadilly. I can't say that
I share his sublime detachment. After all we are in rather an awkward position. A few moments later, as we lie flat on our bellies,
he decides to disregard the Belgians' admonishments and take the
chance of going forward to find the armored car which, for all we
know, might be out of action or even captured.

He tells me to stay where I am and to return to Bruce if he is
not back in five minutes. Before I can voice an opinion he jumps
up and leaves me clutching his rifle and crouching low.

A Belgian sergeant crawls toward me and begs me to fall back
behind their line of fire. I tell him I have orders to stay here
until my Major returns. I believe he thinks we are crazy as he
doubles back to his ditch, shrugging his shoulders disgustedly.

Bullets from across the river are now whizzing through the small
hedge on my right and ricochetting on the stone paving of the
small road, much too close for comfort. And the minutes seem
terribly long as I keep my eyes on my wristwatch.

Five minutes have elapsed. I decide it is time to go for Andrew
and get up to dash in the direction he took. I have not gone twenty
yards when I sight him coming around the corner running toward
me. I don't remember ever having seen a more pleasant sight!
We scramble back to where we left the car and he tells me he has
found the armored car in a very good position and completely in
control of the bridge crossing. He adds that quite a few German
advanced scouts must have found that out too, for the half-destroyed
bridge is strewn with their corpses.

We go to Oplinter to make contact with the Belgian regimental
C.P. which has just been established there. They think that with
our help they will be able to hold the enemy on the Tirlemont-
Gette line providing the Germans are also checked in the south
between here and Jodoigne. As we leave, the Belgian Colonel receives a message. He tells us that one of his companies has just had
a sharp encounter with some enemy forward units at Budingen. We
smile and tell him that we have just come from there and have seen
the fun. We compliment him on the fine bearing of his troops and
part very good friends.

20.45 hrs. We are back in St. Martins. Everyone is tired and hungry so I set out to find a place where we can cook some kind of a meal and eat it in peace. Eventually, after having been turned down by half a dozen householders, I more or less force my way into the last house and make a bargain with the owner for the use of half the stove and the unoccupied dining room. And by 22 hrs. we have had a hot dinner of eggs and tin beef and are lying down on the hard tile floor trying to catch up on sleep.

The Major wakes me up an hour before midnight. The Colonel has just talked to him on the wireless. He wants me to go to the Belgian Battery Commander for information. I walk to the Battery H.Q. which is on the hill just outside the village. The guns are letting loose a heavy barrage. The noise is terrific. I am stopped by a sentry and have some trouble getting to the Commanding Officer who is very busy on the telephone, receiving the sensings from his O.P.

He is very young and smart-looking and he and his staff seem to know their business. He reports that the Belgian positions on the road to St. Trond are holding fast, but that the enemy has occupied Goetsenhoven and the airfield near it. The French D.L.M. and the British armored cavalry, though outnumbered by the German panzer divisions, seem to be holding for the time being a position forming a rough semi-circle between Tirlemont and Jodoigne.

The night is cool and bright with stars. The guns have ceased firing now and, as I walk slowly back to the Squadron C.P., all is silent around me except for an occasional burst of machine-gun fire down in the valley below, along the banks of the Gette, and a muffled rumble of cannon fire coming from the south in the direction of Jodoigne.

FOURTH DAY

Monday, May 13th, 4.30 hrs.

DAWN IS HARDLY breaking when Trooper Machin wakes the Major and me with a bowl of hot tea and some eggs. John joins us. He is bleary-eyed and worn out—he has been on watch since 2 a. m.

As I am busy washing and shaving under the farmyard pump, the Major calls for me. Bruce and Peter have just sent a message asking for gasoline and ammunition. Andrew asks me if I would take the fighting lorry and do the job as I am the only one beside himself who knows the exact positions of the squadron's armored cars. He tells me that I shall be the judge as to how far I can go, once I get on the small road by the Gette, as there my lorry will be in full view of the enemy. He and John bid me farewell and I leave with my carload of gas and ammunition.

6.00 hrs. I have reached our first position in Oplinter. So far so good. Lt. Andrew's troop fills up. As we enter Drieslinter, we are greeted by a continuous crackle of rifle fire coming from across the small river. We forge ahead to get behind cover of a house in the village and I jump out of the lorry to see if there is any harm done. Only one gas can has been punctured. Leaving the lorry behind the house, I proceed on foot to where I had left Peter's troop yesterday. I can see no sign of him, and the Belgian soldiers I encounter can give me no information either. Fifteen minutes are wasted searching along the river and its adjoining farmyards without success. So I return to the lorry and decide to

35

continue on toward Budingen and Bruce's troop. We get there without trouble, hide the lorry in a small farmyard and unload the gasoline and ammunition. Poor Bruce has had a tough night and is haggard. He has not slept a wink as his position is exposed; he cannot relax for a moment.

As we are about to leave, three Junkers, roaring overhead, at about six hundred feet, machine-gun us. We scramble to a deserted pigsty for shelter. My driver doesn't seem eager to get back to the truck, but we must move out of here fast before the Junkers come back again. I succeed in getting him to the truck and we speed to Drieslinter, bouncing along the road at top speed. We get to the village in record time. I tell the driver to hide the car under a tree and to camouflage it with branches. Then I commandeer a Belgium motorcyclist, and we start off towards the river, searching for Peter's troop. Finally I see it on a small dirt road near a shack behind a tiny blown-up road bridge at the narrowest part of the stream, northeast of the village.

The Germans are behind a line of trees about one hundred and fifty yards away. They also seem to have some machine guns in a one-story house just barely visible around the bend of the road. Three wrecked German motor cycles and six dead bodies sprawling in the mud thirty yards ahead of Peter's advanced car prove the effectiveness of his troop's fire.

Smiling and gay as always, Peter welcomes me to his dilapidated lodgings as graciously as a country squire receiving a week-end guest. Even his nearby Boche neighbors have not prevented him from having his morning shave. He is puffing away at the little pipe I gave him one day in Arras, a month—no, ages ago. His No. I car is covering the bridge, No. II is behind the wall of his shack, and No. III is about one hundred yards away to the left, commanding the railroad tracks and the railway bridge which have not been blown up.

Chicken feathers are scattered all over the ground and an appetizing odor of broth emanates from a large iron pot which is setting on some bricks over burning embers. Peter's troop will not go hungry. Their morale is excellent. Peter has also found some bottles of mineral water which he insists I must take back with me. When I tell him I am running short of our favorite pipe tobacco, he dives inside his armored car and emerges triumphantly with a pound tin which he also forces on me. I notice then that a fuzzy plush monkey has been fixed on the hood of his car. It perches there solemnly with a silly worried expression on its face. It is a prime mascot for Troop No. II.

As we laugh and joke and walk around in full view of the enemy, I can't help wondering if some Boche beyond the river isn't watching with bewilderment all these touching domestic scenes through his Zeiss glasses.

9.00 hrs. Squadron Headquarters calls Peter over the radio phone. They want to know if I have been seen. I answer for myself and tell the Major that the lorry is safely hidden in the village and that the supplies are being brought here by hand.

An hour later I am back in the lorry on our way to Squadron H. Q. Belgian antitank guns placed on the south side of the road are hammering at an enemy concentration on the east bank of the Gette. The Germans have brought up some field guns, for as we enter Drieslinter three 105-mm. shrapnels whine overhead and explode with terrific cracks over the Hoelden road, which we must take. This seems to give wings to our lorry for it screeches around the turn on two wheels and flies up the hill towards St. Martins. We reach there at 11.00 hrs.

At 13.00 hrs. the Major and I go to visit the Belgian Battery Commander. His guns are firing at Goetsenhoven and on a long line of enemy lorries coming up the road leading to it. A squadron of Junkers flies over us and bombs the Tirlemont-Louvain highway. We can see smoke and dust rising from it for more than two miles. The bombers wheel around and circle twice over our village and the batteries which have stopped firing. I hold my breath waiting for the bombs, but none come. Andrew grins at me. Our crossroad is safe after all.

News from the south is bad. The German tanks have rammed a hole through the D.L.M.'s defense around Jandraine. The Major says we may have to withdraw lest we be cut off from Louvain. We take the staff car and go down to see what is happening on the bank of the Gette river. At Oplinter all is quiet,

The Belgian commander is optimistic. He probably has not learned what we know.

We continue on to Drieslinter and walk to Peter's outpost to find, as we near it, that he and a Belgian patrol are heavily engaged with the opposing force in the house across the river. We hug the hedges and dodging from tree to tree reach the armored cars.

Two wounded soldiers of the Belgian patrol are lying in the field across the stream. A German machine gun is making it difficult to rescue them. Peter, rifle in hand, is shooting at the bushes about two hundred yards away from which the enemy fire is coming. Bullets are spattering against the shack behind which we stand. The Major and I grab two rifles and run to take cover behind what remains of the bridge stone parapet. On our right a Belgian officer is blasting away at the small house with the anti-tank gun. Another group of Belgians, squatting behind a heavy machine gun on our left, fire short bursts in the direction of the railroad tracks.

Four men, two Belgians and two volunteers from Peter's group, succeed in crossing the deep gully under the blown-up bridge and worm their way up to the wounded men. Moving cautiously along the hedge which hides them from the enemy, they dart across the field and drag the men to the safety of a ditch. Then, inch by inch, yard by yard, they crawl back to us, dragging the two unconscious bodies while bullets whistle overhead and toss up tufts of grass around them. Twenty minutes after they have left, we help them up the gully and carry the wounded to a Belgian field ambulance which has driven up behind Peter's armored car. Both men are hit in the belly. They look as if they were dead.

15.30 hrs. The firing has subsided. The Major decides to move on to visit Bruce's troop. We return to our car and speed to Budingen where we find the armored cars of No. 1 troop in the same positions as yesterday. Bruce looks completely exhausted. He has had no sleep for sixty-six hours. His face is gray with caked sweat and dust, his eyelids heavy and swollen. His men are no better off than he. They have not been as lucky as Peter's troop, having no place in which they can rest and eat. The

Major, after looking them over and talking to Bruce, does not think he can leave the troop there much longer. I make Bruce drink some good wine which I always carry with me and force him to eat some biscuits and chocolate. This bucks him up a bit. After a few minutes, we leave them to their lonely and dangerous task and turn the car toward Tirlemont.

As we are nearing Drieslinter at full speed, a motorbike lying in the middle of the road forces us to stop. Getting out of the car to drag it out of the way, we catch sight of its driver, a Belgian cavalryman, lying on his belly in a field of clover on the side of the road. When he sees us, he points upward and back of us. We promptly turn around and at once understand why he had incontinently abandoned his motorcycle.

Screeching down from the sky, five Stukas are diving straight at us. Three leaps carry me to the middle of the field. I nose-dive into the green clover. I flatten down, my heart thumping like a bass drum—1, 2, 3, 4, 5, 6 bombs hurtle down, screaming. A deafening noise. Smoke. Blinding flashes. The earth rocks under me. Then the roar of the planes passes and I stagger to my feet feeling rather sick. Fifty yards away to my left I am happy to see Andrew waving to me. Fred, our driver, scrambles out of the ditch. The Belgian soldier walks slowly back to his motorcycle. The Junkers have missed the road; all the bombs have fallen quite near, but on the other side of it. The smoking craters are in a straight line about twenty yards apart. We reach the car and find that the left door is damaged. It won't shut, but somehow we fix it.

Andrew, after taking one look at Fred, who is too shaky to be of any use, gets into the driver's seat. We hurry to Oplinter where we pay a visit to the Belgian Colonel and find at his C.P. the Chief of Staff of the Belgian Cavalry Corps. He confirms that the French D.L.M. has been forced to abandon the position it held this morning south of Tirlemont. This looks bad as it means that the Germans might now push up from the south to gain access to the Tirlemont-Louvain highway and cut us off. We lose no time in getting back to St. Martins to report to our Colonel by wireless.

17.00 hrs. The Major sends an armored car commanded by young Andrew, who has been relieved from his position in Oplinter, on a patrol through Tirlemont to find out if he can see any signs of the enemy this side of the Gette south of the Louvain road.

I decide to take Trooper Machin on an expedition of our own to try to buy bread and eggs. These useful and very rare commodities are such a welcome addition to our iron rations, which are all we carry in the way of food.

In every house we enter we find the people packing and getting ready to leave. Most of the women are in tears. I try to comfort them and reassure them the best I can. In a bakery a young woman, with three small children, clings to my tunic and begs me to advise her what to do and to tell her if it is true that the Germans are already in St. Trond. If I tell them the truth, that the enemy is only about three miles away, the whole village will be thrown into a panic. So I just smile at them all and say that they shouldn't believe rumors and that, anyway, as long as the British Lancers are in the village they have nothing to worry about. This white lie gains us two dozen eggs and three loaves of delicious bread.

Young Andrew pulls up in his car coming back from Tirlemont. He reports that he has seen Belgian troops dribbling back from the St. Trond road and he understands that the Cavalry Corps is withdrawing to Louvain. He has been heavily shelled at the eastern end of the town, the gun fire apparently coming from the south. This means that German field artillery has moved up in that direction, and I am sent to the Belgian battery commander to learn what he knows about it. John comes with me.

As we enter the small room in the farm house on the hill outside the village which is the battery C.P., we find the officers too busy even to talk. We stand quietly in a corner of the room while orders are transmitted to the gun positions. Then, all of a sudden, there is a rumbling and a roar. Hell breaks loose. The house shakes. The windows are blown open. Twelve 75's have opened fire simultaneously and are barking like a pack of monster metallic wild dogs, belching fire and sending red hot steel hurtling and whistling through the air. The noise is deafening. A

Belgian officer scribbles something on a scrap of paper and hands it to me. I read "4 x 12." That means four shots from each gun.

In a few seconds the guns are silent. The forty-eight shots have been fired. Soon after the telephone rings, reporting direct hits on the enemy. Trucks have been seen blown to bits on the Guetsenhoven airfield and their crews stampeding for shelter. This information is transmitted to the gun emplacements with an order to resume firing.

"Now we can talk," says the battery commander, who is more used to this terrific din than we are. Screaming into his ears, we tell him the object of our visit. He says that he has just been ordered to cover the retreat of the troops defending Tirlemont by laying a heavy barrage ahead of them. The evacuation will start at dusk and should go on very rapidly. He and his battery will try to withdraw later after firing every shell in their caissons.

John tells him that we will protect him with a troop of armored cars. Young Andrew's troop is to have this job and it takes up its position a few hundred yards ahead of the different gun emplacements on the narrow country road which winds down toward Tirlemont. Bruce and Peter call up to say that the Belgian troops around them are withdrawing. They want to know what to do. They are told by the Major to stick it out until further orders.

20.00 hrs. Hot soup, bread and butter and three soft-boiled eggs each! After this mighty banquet, Andrew advises me to snatch a few minutes' sleep if I can as he feels we will have a busy night. So John and I find an old tattered mattress. We lie down on it and promptly pass out. Two and one-half hours later the Major walks into the room and wakes us. Orders from headquarters are that we are to start the withdrawal at 23.00 hrs.

Beyond the village, the 75's are firing away at top speed, using up their ammunition. The noise is terrific, but exhilarating. The glow of blazing houses in Tirlemont lights up the whole horizon. I am told that while I was sleeping peacefully wave after wave of bombers had blasted the little town, setting it on fire. Even now loud explosions rock the earth as Belgian ammunition dumps a mile away are blown up.

I climb the hill to get a better view and hear the rattle of machine guns down on the Gette. Budingen appears to be on fire, too. Bruce and Peter are still down there. Silhouetted against the scarlet horizon one hundred yards ahead of me, I can see one of young Andrew's cars, watching and waiting.

Back in the village, the Major tells me that he has ordered both troops on the Gette to withdraw. I am relieved. The squadron's rendezvous is at Lovenjoel on the Louvain road. I am to ride ahead in the staff car with the fighting lorry behind me and John's armored car following. My orders are to move off at once. In pitch darkness, without lights, we proceed carefully along narrow torn-up country roads and paths towards the Louvain highway which we reach about midnight, three miles west of Tirlemont.

An appalling sight greets us there. Enemy bombers have reduced this wide and lovely road, lined with tall trees, to havoc and desolation. Trucks, large passenger buses, private cars, some still on fire, are strewn over it. One huge holiday bus has been blown up beside a wrecked house, its front wheels resting on what remains of the roof. It is still flaming like a gigantic pyre, casting a red glow on the pools of blood and the mutilated bodies which are lying about it.

We make slow headway, avoiding the bomb craters and obstacles in our path. To the left of the road on the railroad tracks a train is ablaze, lighting up the countryside. Finally we reach the hamlet of Lovenjoel, which consists of about a dozen houses among tall trees on both sides of the road.

FIFTH DAY

THE MAJOR AND the remainder of our H. Q. troops' armored cars join us, shortly followed by Peter and Bruce and their troops. The nine cars and their crews line up under the leafy trees. We sit on doorsteps and on the ground, waiting. After awhile the Colonel drives up in his command car and we join him for a conference in an empty barn. He issues his orders by the glimmer of a candle-stub and gives us a brief resumé of the tactical situation. News from the south is not good. The enemy is pushing forward with at least two tank divisions. The lighter French D.L.M.'s, having taken severe punishment, are falling back towards Gembloux and the main position on the Dyle and the Meuse rivers. Though greatly outnumbered, they are fighting every yard of the way and causing heavy casualties. North of Tirlemont the Belgian cavalry corps, as we already know, is also falling back. The High Command, fearing that this situation might create a dangerous gap, wants us to keep a steady watch on all enemy movements and try to retard him, if possible, with the help of two divisional cavalry regiments, until we retire behind the infantry which is busy fortifying Louvain.

"After that you will probably be given a rest," adds the Colonel. We salute and file out of the barn, leaving the Major with the Colonel for further conference.

After the Colonel has left, the Major tells us that we are to

43

remain here until young Andrew and his troop arrive, then move
to our new position on the Loo Ridge, which rises two hundred
and fifty feet above and east of Louvain where we shall join the
13/18 Hussars.   Their light tanks are to help us in our task of
watching and holding the enemy as long as we can.

The Major advises each of us to try to get some rest while we
can.   Bruce and Peter climb into their armored cars and John
and I seek shelter in an empty house.   The front door is battered
in and the rooms are in a state of complete disorder.   Evidently
the house has either been occupied by troops or visited by looters;
the result is usually the same.

While we look around for a clean place to lie down, an ever-
increasing drone of enemy bombers fills the air, shortly followed
by several bomb crashes about a quarter of a mile up the road.
John suggests the cellar.   It would not give us any protection
if a direct hit were made on the house, but it sounds like a
good idea anyway, so we walk down the slimy steps, groping
our way in total darkness.   We settle down on the damp floor,
sitting with our backs to the stone wall.   We are so exhausted
that we fall into a deep slumber.

After awhile I wake up feeling very chilly and notice a peculiar
sweet sickening stench which is so insistent that it prevents me
from going back to sleep.   I flick on my flashlight to look at my
watch and see revealed the mangled body of a woman, lying in
a pool of coagulated blood a few inches away from me.   Her
left leg is cut off from the thigh down.   Feeling violently ill,
I jump to my feet.   As I run towards the stairs, I stumble over
a large wooden clothes bucket half filled with pinkish water—
and the women's leg!   Three leaps take me to the top of the
stairs and the road outside.   I walk up and down inhaling the
cold night air.   I decide to leave John to his blissful sleep.

All is quiet.   The sky is empty, save for thousands of stars
shining brightly in the cloudless sky.   Andrew is asleep in the
staff car.   Most of the squadron are snoring.   Soon I hear in the
distance a rumbling from the direction of Tirlemont.   In a moment I see the guns of the Belgian 18th Light Artillery, who were
in position at St. Martins, pass by.   The Commanding Officer

stops his car when he recognizes me and tells me that they were able to effect their dangerous withdrawal with clockwork precision and had lost only one gun. I compliment him on his achievement and he asks me to thank Andrew for the help which young Andrew's troop has given him in his difficult task.

Five minutes after he has disappeared in the direction of Louvain, Andrew's troop drives up. I wake the Major and young Andrew makes his report. The gunner of his forward armored car has been hit. The Major orders John's gunner to take his place and I am temporarily to substitute for John's gunner in the rear link car.

3.30 hrs. We are off, heading up the hill towards Loo on the donkey-back ridge which rises steeply between the Louvain-Diest and Louvain-Tirlemont highways. John, who has had a good sleep, is either totally unaware of the corpse that had companioned us in the cellar or else is prevented by British reticence from mentioning it. We remain silent as we ride through the night standing up in the turret of his car between the Bren and Boys guns.

We reach Loo at 4.00 hrs. Bruce's and Peter's troops move off towards the advanced position near Lubeek. Tim, who has just returned from leave in England and rejoined the squadron today, has taken over young Andrew's troop and leaves with them. 13/18th Hussars are already established on the Ridge. Paul de Rosiere, who is the liaison of that squadron, comes and chats with me.

The ever-resourceful Machin helps me force our way into a boarded up and empty *estaminet,* which we decide to use as headquarters. Then, after exploring several hay lofts, he returns with his steel helmet filled with eggs. Soon hot water is boiling and a breakfast of eggs and tea are set before us. I try to compel young Andrew to eat a little, but the boy is so done in that he can't keep his eyes open; his head keeps falling on the table. Finally he goes to sleep with his face in the eggs.

I can hardly stay awake myself and lie down on the narrow wooden bench in the café with my head on my gas mask, and sleep. Machin, lying on the brick floor under my bench, does the same.

I wake at 5.30 feeling much better. Sunshine is streaming through the closed wooden shutters. Young Andrew is still fast asleep in the same position, his face smeared with egg yolk. I walk into the courtyard, wash my face in cool pump water and shave.

The air is filled with the roar of engines as squadron after squadron of German Stuka bombers and Heinkels sweep by over us, then circle and plunge one after the other above the old historic city of Louvain, pulling out of their screaming dives only when they have dropped their load of explosives. The earth trembles under the impact of their bombs, while the whole city below us, its ancient buildings fast becoming piles of stone and rubble, disappears from sight under a thick cloud of black smoke and dust.

We quickly mount some of our Bren guns on wooden posts and blaze away at the Stukas as they go by. Yet they keep coming on in a seemingly endless stream, roaring low over our heads. Either they don't see our armored cars and trucks, which are very well camouflaged and covered with straw to make them look like haystacks, or their mission is to bomb Louvain only. Anyway, they leave us alone and disdainfully ignore our Bren guns which are harmlessly popping at them.

After watching this spectacle for awhile, I return to the *estaminet* where I find a sewing basket left by the fleeing owners. Helping myself to needle and thread, I sit in a corner and consolidate a few of my loose buttons while waiting for orders.

Andrew asks me to go with him in the staff car immediately on a reconnaissance toward Lubeek as he is not quite satisfied with the positions that Bruce's and Peter's troops have taken. Tim is also believed to be in a bad spot. As we depart, the aerial carrousel is still in full swing and Fred, our driver, seems much more concerned with the enemy aircraft than with his driving. So Andrew decides to take over the wheel and orders Fred to the back seat where he can watch the planes to his heart's content through the rear window.

The widening dirt track on which we are driving and which follows the ridge from Loo to Lubeek is bumpy and dry. Clouds of dust kicked up by our car make us uncomfortably conspicuous to the planes flying above. Every few hundred yards we pass light tanks of the 13/18th hidden behind hedges and stacks of wheat. Andrew drives on unmindful of the threatening Heinkels, some of which are so low that we can see the short flame-bursts of their machine guns as they dive toward us.

I am so nervous that I keep my hand on the door handle ready to jump out. As for poor Fred, he is green in the face. But Andrew, who I have discovered does not know the meaning of the word fear, merely grins and drives on with that mad look in his eye that I know so well by now, and don't like much when I happen to be in a position to be concerned with its consequences.

We eventually reach Lubeek and see no sign of our armored cars. Turning left, we drive toward the Diest road and, finding no sign of life there either, we return to Lubeek, go through it and, swinging right after the last houses, follow a cart-track which climbs to the top of a steep hill crowned by a clump of pine trees. There we can clearly see in the soft soil fresh tracks of the distinctive tread of our armored cars and in the distance the dust raised by a column of German armored vehicles which are advancing toward Lubeek from Attenrode.

We hastily get back to our car and drive down to Lubeek. As we round into the main square we nearly bump into Tim's armored car. He gives us the new positions taken up by No. I and No. II troop and also that of his troop. They are now all holding good, well-concealed positions on high ground from which they can watch and report the enemy's advance. Tim believes that they will make contact with the enemy within a half hour at most.

We turn the staff car back towards Loo and reach it by 8.30.

10.00 hrs. Tim reports on the wireless that he has just had a skirmish with some advance elements and is holding out all right. The firing of all his guns at once seems to have surprised the German column further back as it has stopped and appears to be trying to turn around to reach shelter or to await reinforcements. He has seen no tanks yet. One of his men is wounded.

Thirty minutes later we get bad news from our right flank.

The 15/19th Hussars, who are holding a position astride the Tirlemont-Louvain highway report that they are being driven in. They have sustained severe losses. Their Colonel orders withdrawal. Andrew is fighting mad. He calls up our Colonel to report this and afterward walks with me to the C.P. of the 13/18th to find out what plans they have made. When we get there, we find them in the midst of preparations for a hasty withdrawal, like their colleagues of the 15/19th.

I hear Andrew try to persuade their C.O. to stay a while longer, but orders are orders and he is not successful. Finally he stomps out of their C.P. grumbling that the 12th Lancers will jolly well show these blankety-blank Hussars that they are not afraid of the adjectived Huns.

One by one under Andrew's stony glare the Light Cavalry Tanks rumble by leaving the village on their way downhill toward Louvain and comparative safety. Lt Mera and Paul De Rosiere, their liaison officers, jump out of their Bren carriers to shake hands with me and wish me Godspeed.

By midday Squadron A 12 Lancers is alone on the narrow Loo ridge. Bruce is retreating towards us and we can see his dust in the distance. Peter who has been practically surrounded is fighting his way back, and Tim has moved to a new position from where he can see a great number of German tanks entering Lovenjoel, where we were only a few hours ago.

Our Colonel phones that B Squadron, which was on our left in a position similar to ours on the parallel ridge which lies between the Louvain-Diest and the Louvain-Arrashot roads, is retreating toward Louvain. He tells Andrew to use his own judgment, but to keep in mind that if we linger too long we may be cut off from the only bridge to Louvain.

Andrew stubbornly decides to hang on a little longer, but orders the advanced troops to start falling back toward Loo. John says nothing, just looks at me. And Machin slyly suggests that we may still have sauerkraut for dinner.

Tim reports later that the Germans have passed through Korbeek and are now less than three miles from Louvain. Bruce's wireless has been put out of action so he sends one of his D.R.'s to report it. Andrew orders them to return to us at once.

We all gather in Loo. Andrew sends Peter and his troop down the hill toward the Louvain Bridge on the Diest road, with orders to report if the road is clear. Peter soon reports from the Diest road that he has seen some German motor cycle scouts and has fired on them. Andrew directs him to proceed to the bridge at once and to warn the engineers there not to blow it up until we have passed.

14.00 hrs. Bruce and his troop leave, then Tim, followed by the H. Q. Troop with Andrew and young Andrew, the fighting lorry and staff car. John's armored car closes the march. I am still acting as his gunner and I swing the turret around to face the rear. We soon reach the Diest highway and find the crumpled bodies of the German motorcyclists killed by Peter's gunners sprawling in the dust near the crossroad. German bombers are still diving and zooming up again over the bridge we have to cross. They seem to have decided to destroy it and cut us off. I cannot say that I am happy over the situation. Still, there is nothing for me to do but to stand up and try to hide my feelings while the armored car speeds on.

14.30 hrs. The whole squadron has crossed the bridge. It is defended by the Welsh guards. They look well-armed and determined, and it is good to see them.

Andrew asks John and me to stay behind near the bridge until it is blown up and then to rejoin the squadron at Oppen near Brussels. All houses beside the Dyle are banked with sandbags and bristling with light and heavy machine guns. Two well-camouflaged and well-protected antitank guns are set up on the right and left sides of the street at the bridgehead.

Unmindful of the bombing, a young subaltern of the Welsh guards dashes across the street to bring us bottles of beer and lemonade. Very welcome; our throats are parched and we have had nothing to eat since five this morning. Now and again when a bomb crashes too near we have to dive inside our car. We are told that since this morning more than sixty men have been killed by the bombing.

The same question is on everybody's lips: Where are our planes? What are they doing? Why are they not sent here to protect us?

Lord Freddy Cambridge, the cousin of the King, and my friend of the camera incident, sends a messenger to John and me with a bottle of old brandy and a funny note explaining why he is too busy now to help us drink it. We scribble a few words of thanks and best wishes and are about to despatch it when the rattle of two heavy machine guns breaking into action near us sends everyone helter-skelter to their battle stations. At the same moment the bridge is blown up with a terrific blast, right under the wheels of a platoon of German motorcyclists who are sent flying skyward. The explosion is so loud and shattering that it knocks me down to the bottom of the car. John's pipe flies out of his mouth. Scrambling to our feet, we pull Lord Freddy's messenger up onto the car and speed off to a safer spot around the next corner while bricks, stones and scraps of iron come crashing down on the paved street all around us.

It was exactly 16.00 hrs. when the bridge blew up. Now that it is gone, our job is finished and we drive off through the ruins of Louvain with a feeling of relief. The fighting is up to the infantry now and we of the 12th Lancers are heading for food, sleep, and maybe a much-needed bath!

All the squadron's armored cars and the trucks from our transport echelon waiting for us at Oppen are hidden under the thick foliage of the beautiful trees in the park of a chateau belonging to Comte de Grune. The house is large, modern and well-furnished.

Oppen is only a few miles east of Brussels on the northern edge of the lovely Soygnes Forest. It reminds me of Sunningdale near Windsor Park in England or the North Shore of Long Island. Wealthy *Bruxellois* go there for weekends.

I am much too tired to appreciate these luxurious surroundings and I just manage to climb up the stairs to a tiny room on the second floor which has been assigned to me. There I find Stevens, my batman, who has prepared a wonderful-looking bed for me on a narrow couch. The last time I saw Stevens was a week ago when he helped me pack my things to go to Paris on leave. So much has happened since then!

He is a regular army soldier and a pukka batman with a dry sense of humor and the rare knack of knowing when to remain silent. He helps me to undress and to pull off the heavy cavalry boots which have been on my swollen feet and tired legs for four days and nights, ever since last Saturday morning. Deftly he unpacks my light kit while I fall into a deep and much-needed sleep.

I wake up at 20.00 hrs. and join the others in the dining room. We are all in pajamas and still so exhausted that we just sit there and munch our food in a sort of daze without saying a word. It feels good though to sit at a table and have warm soup, roast meat and vegetables. Best of all, God only knows why, none of us is missing.

After coffee, we all return to our bedrooms for more sleep. Right now our only ambition is to sleep—to sleep long and hard. Just sleep for hours.

Wednesday, May 15th, 4.30 hours

A LONG AND STEADILY increasing roar of engines from what sounds like at least fifty bombers wakes me at 4.30 hrs. The short staccato of machine guns follows immediately right under my window. As I jump up to find out what is going on, I can see tracer bullets speeding skyward as wave after wave of the large black bombers in perfect formation fly over the park, apparently headed for Brussels. They are so low that their black crosses, outlined in white, are plainly visible. Other Bren guns join in the fun, their bullets, flying straight at the passing Junkers, draw sharp lines of fire which streak across the grey sky of dawn.

One of the planes breaks off from the others. It makes a steep left turn followed by a steady stream of bullets from all our guns. Smoke is pouring out of it. One, two, three of its crew bail out, their parachutes widening into big white mushrooms while the abandoned plane crashes with a loud explosion on the crest of a hill about a mile away and bursts into flame.

Looking down, I see Andrew in his pajamas order a sergeant and two men armed with rifles to hop into the fighting lorry and speed after the plane's crew.

Three loud cheers rise from the park. The boys are celebrating their victory. I go back to bed.

Stevens wakes me up at 7 with a cup of tea and tells me that the men did not bring back the German flyers after all. The

Jerries were dead before they landed, riddled with bullets from a machine gun.

Orders are to move at 8.00. Stevens packs my kit and I run downstairs where I find Peter and Bruce eating a few biscuits left behind by our cook. They tell me that the Major wants me to leave at once with John in the staff car and go to Lennick St. Kwintens southwest of Brussels to prepare the billeting.

On the way, John tells me that A. Squadron has had the honor to be chosen by General Gort as his special guard. It seems G.H.Q. is highly pleased with the squadron's good showing on the Gette and at Loo and that for the next twenty-four hours at least we are to provide for the safety of the Commander-in-Chief's advanced C.P. against airborne troops and enemy agents.

St. Kwintens is a large aggregation of snug little bourgeois houses, too near Brussels to be by itself either a village or small town. As is usual in Belgium, it has an elaborate city hall facing a large paved main square around which stand most of the stores and cafes. It lies between Ninove-Brussels and the Halle-Brussels highways, about ten miles south of the Belgian capital.

No one there seems to be aware that the British Commander-in-Chief has established his headquarters in the small chateau which lies surrounded by stately trees only a few hundred yards away from the square.

It takes me at least three hours to find sheds, barns and garages in which to hide all the squadron's armored cars and the trucks and lorries of the transport troop. Then, I have to find suitable billets for the men and the officers. Just as I have about finished my task, exhausted by the heat and the constant running around, Andrew and the whole squadron draw up on the village square. I have to start over again showing the troops the different lodgings I have found for them.

As usual, they are all dissatisfied and, to finish it off, Andrew tells me that I have to find a house where the officers can be billeted as he has orders that we must all be together and on constant alert. Little does he know that I have been trying all morning to find such a house and that I have been assured that it is impossible. This is a word that Andrew doesn't like. So I

shove off again, waved on cheerfully by Bruce and Peter who are
sitting on the sidewalk of the main square under the blazing sun,
hoping for a bottle of cold beer and a sandwich. It is past 1
p. m. now and the cup of tea and biscuit which we had at 7 this
morning seem very far away.

The civilians are not particularly helpful. This rich little town
so near the capital has not yet fully realized that there is a war
on, and that the enemy is hammering at the line of the Dyle,
which is only about fifteen miles away. The news they have had
so far on the radio has been rather on the optimistic side,
victories even being intimated. So it is no wonder that the
people are bewildered by our appearance; our faces grey with
dust and drawn with fatigue, our uniforms dirty, our armored
cars caked with clay and showing the marks of enemy bullets.
It does not seem possible to them that they are actually seeing
men who have just fought the Germans and who have been
under fire. They look upon us with curiosity mingled with distrust, regarding us more like intruders who have come to disturb
their peaceful habits and deplete their stores than as allies who
are trying to save them from destruction. Some of them, too,
have very definite sympathies toward the invaders. These mostly
belong to the Rexist Party and we have a list of them. They bear
watching.

All of the shops and *estaminets* have been closed by the local
authorities. This makes it hard for us. But I succeed in getting
into a grocery store through a back entrance which Machin has
discovered and in cajoling the owner into selling me some food
for the officers and men.

She is tall, buxom, pink-cheeked, a friendly type of woman
and she takes pity on us. When I tell her about my troubles in
finding an empty house, she informs me that there is a small villa
on the main square which has been abandoned by its proprietor,
an old lady, this morning. I go there immediately only to find
it locked, its shutters closed. A neighbor, aroused by my banging
on the door, tells me that the keys have been taken by the old
lady's nephew who lives in a village seven miles away. I hop
into the staff car and return an hour later with the keys.

We move in. The house is small and there is only one bed-
room on the first floor with a double bed and a mattress. I allo-
cate this room to Andrew and John. The other officers and myself
will sleep on the floor of what was the dining room and which
is now bare of furniture. There is also a tiny kitchen with some
pots and pans and another small room, also devoid of furniture,
where we shall mess. At the back of the house, a walled-in
orchard and a small flower garden will provide us with privacy
and an agreeable resting place. The Major returns from a visit
to the Colonel. When he sees the house he pats me on the back
and seems delighted with the arrangements.

One troop has been ordered to place its armored cars in
strategic positions around the main square, hidden in the shade
as much as possible. All the other troops are to take their turn
during the coming night. Peter and his troop have the first watch.
The others strip and bathe under the garden pump. The water
is cold and refreshing. A large wooden bucket makes a very good
tub and we splash about minus our clothes while German observation planes circle ominously above us.

Taking Machin along, I go out to do some shopping for dinner.
All we find are some cauliflowers, canned peas, and potatoes, but
my grocerlady friend, kind-hearted soul that she is, lets me
have a few slices of a delicious ham which is her private property
and which is not on sale. She invites me into her living room to
hear the new radio. But I am not allowed to listen very long as
she talks continually, telling me that her husband has been mobilized
and that she hopes the war will soon be over as she is already
beginning to feel lonesome. I eventually manage to break away
by promising to return later on in the evening.

Our Colonel drops in for a drink before dinner. He tells us
that the High Command is well satisfied with the 12th Lancers
and gives us news of what the other squadrons have accomplished
since May 11th. B Squadron has destroyed several German tanks
and one troop leader has made a wonderful record extricating his
cars from what appeared to be a hopeless position. He adds that
the German aircraft have been pounding the Dyle position through
the day and that the Guards have suffered severe losses at Louvain.

Our friend, Lord Frederick Cambridge, has been killed! Up north the battle in Holland is over; the Dutch army has laid down its arms. This complete elimination of our ally in so short a time—five days—fills us with gloom. We eat an early dinner and lie down on a wooden floor in the next room.

I have been asleep for about two hours when I am awakened by a loud crash and the feeling that the house is about to fall down on top of me. Peter, who is lying not far from me, sits up with a start, and so do the others, as the door swings open and the windows are shattered by new and violent explosions. Several machine guns are firing. We run out into the square. There is a bright moon and no clouds. Black bombers are flying over the small town.

One bomb falls on a railroad crossing three hundred yards away. Others are scattered to right and left. We feel helpless with no other defense than our ineffectual Bren guns and can only hope for the best. By good luck, no bombs are dropped in the direction of the chateau where General Gort is staying.

A few minutes later all is quiet again and we return to our hard beds to try to sleep. Peter and Bruce take a swig from their flasks, I share a bottle of beer with Tim and we argue for awhile as to what has happened to our anti-aircraft guns. We have neither seen nor heard one since the battle started. One of us suggests that they are probably protecting the higher staffs far back of the lines, and there are not enough of them to send up here to protect the men at the front. As this discussion is leading us nowhere rapidly, I fold up my coat as a pillow and am soon fast asleep.

SEVENTH DAY

Thursday, May 16th, 6 hours

THE GERMAN DAWN patrol is already over us in huge waves. I count more than sixty Heinkels and Junkers. Our orders arrive at 6. We are to be ready to move on one hour's notice. Stevens packs my kit and fills my haversack with tins of food from my reserve. I walk out into the streets with Machin in search of bread, and we are lucky enough to find a baker who is willing to sell us at a high price some loaves which he has just taken out of the oven. I distribute them to the troop leaders, together with bottles of claret which I have succeeded in getting hold of.

Walking back to our lodgings, I meet John who is walking up the street with H.R.H. the Duke of Gloucester. Prince Henry is in the best of moods. He had his first real taste of war last night. His house having been bombed, he lost nearly all his kit and had to move to another billet. He is a real soldier and looks it, and I understand when I see him why he is so much liked and admired in the British Army.

8.00 hrs. A dispatch rider drives up at full speed from G.H.Q. asking that the French liaison officer report there at once. Much excited speculation goes on while I smarten up, dust my boots, and put on my helmet and chinstrap. Everyone feels sure that I am about to attend some historic conference between General Gort and some high French general—perhaps General Gamelin.

I walk anxiously toward the small chateau where I am re-

59

ceived immediately and ushered into a long room filled with tables on which huge maps are spread. General Gort is standing in a corner speaking to the Duke of Gloucester and a Colonel of his staff. I click my heels, salute, and stand at attention. A young Major asks my name and if I am the liaison officer sent by Squadron A, 12th Lancer. After giving me a pleasant nod, Lord Gort picks up several maps and walks out to his car with the Colonel of his staff. Prince Henry gets into another car and they are off for the front where the situation is far from good and where the Commander-in-Chief is going to have a conference with the Generals commanding the I and II Corps.

After they have gone, I am told what is expected of me. I attend to it at once, and when I leave the advance G.H.Q. an hour later, everyone seems very happy over the very simple job I have accomplished and a staff officer thanks me profusely. It all boiled down to this. The owner of the chateau disliked to have a staff of British officers in his house so he proceeded—or rather Madame did—to inaugurate a blockade of a special kind on the British guests. She retired all the pots and pans from the kitchen and locked the door leading to the coal cellar. The natural consequence was that the General's French chef was unable to cook any sort of meal! Hence the hurried call for my services. The Commander-in-Chief had had no breakfast.

It would have been easier to settle the whole matter had it been possible to tell the unwilling host and hostess that their guests were none other than Viscount Gort and his staff. But that was entirely out of the question. In the end, when I left the chateau and the coal cellar was wide open; the pots and pans were back in the kitchen, each on its own hook; the French chef was beaming; Madame had dried her tears and was smiling happily once again—and, most important of all, G.H.Q. was to have some lunch!

When I return to the squadron, everyone asks me what has happened, but I refuse to tell and assume the mysterious air of one who has learned a state secret and must guard it with his life.

11.00 hrs. The Colonel has just left the squadron. He brought bad news. The British I Corps' right has withdrawn behind the river Lesne. The French army on our right has fallen back. The Germans have succeeded in forcing their way across the Meuse river. Namur has fallen to the enemy. A battle is in progress at Gembloux and the German armored division has broken through the French defense there also. If this advance is not checked, the enemy should reach the Brussels-Charleroi highway this evening. We are to wait for further orders, but may be asked to march at any minute. Our probable line of battle will be southeast of Waterloo.

We all sit down for a snack and a bottle of beer. The cooks and batmen have left with our transport echelon which has received orders to rejoin regimental headquarters.

16.30 hrs. Orders arrive to march at once and to proceed to Rode St. Genese; the final rendezvous is situated at a point about three kilometers west of the Brussels-Charleroi road north of Waterloo. Andrew tells me that we shall probably be used as support of a French division and most likely fight all night. I clamber up into John's armored car and we are off.

We cross the Senette River and the Brussels-Charleroi Canal. The heavy rumble of artillery on the front ahead of us has died down. The sky is dotted with German aircraft. Light bombers, heavy bombers, fighter Messerschmitts circle over the entire countryside searching for targets. Unchallenged, they fly low, their engines idling. Some of them insultingly make barrel rolls and loops over our heads. This display is tremendously disheartening to all of us, and we cannot help wondering what has happened to our airforce.

We reach Rode St. Genese. Heavy British infantry tanks are thundering down the narrow street coming in our direction. As they pass by, I am amused to read some of the names which are painted in white on them: "Gamelin," "Garbo," "Gorgonzola." The tank corps men are standing in the turrets and wave at us.

I am watching the sky above us when I see five Stukas, which have been flying over on our right, suddenly make a steep left glide. With screaming engines they swoop towards us and I stand spellbound for an instant as I see their bombs start straight for us. John, who is reading his map, is totally unconscious of what is going on, and I drag him down into the cockpit as the first high explosive bursts up the street. The armored car rocks like a dinghy as each second brings a new explosion, blasting house after house in a straight line all the way down the left side of the street. Without slackening speed for a moment the tanks keep rolling on amid the crashing timber and falling brick and, when I look up a few seconds later, I can see the last one disappear around the bend in the direction of Halle.

None of our cars has been hit, so we move off and turn to the right into a small dirt road which leads us away from the burning village.

18.00 hrs. The squadron is well hidden under the trees of a small oval-shaped wood in the middle of a large field, two hundred yards from a small road and opposite a large private estate which appears to be a convent, enclosed in a high stone wall. The wood is about one hundred yards wide and three hundred long. Our armored cars are sheltered along its eastern edge in the shade under the thick branches of tall and leafy oak trees. We are quite invisible from the air, but the deep tracks that our heavy cars have dug through the field can be seen from above and might invite trouble. Bren guns are set up as anti-aircraft protection at both ends of the wood and the Major orders the crew to rest and make tea.

The Colonel arrives. He leads us to the sunny side of the wood away from the men. There we sit under the trees with our maps stretched out on the grass while he gives us the latest information.

The I and II corps of the B.E.F. are withdrawing behind Brussels. The French on our right are falling back. The Germans have already reached Nivelles and are pushing forward in a northwesterly direction in order to encircle Brussels. A gap has been created between the two armies, and just now there seems to be no organized infantry units between the advancing enemy and us except some elements of a French division which have had very rough going and are presumably in bad shape.

The squadron is to move off at 20.00 hrs., to take up a line on the ridge overlooking a narrow valley along a road between Mont

St. John, south of Waterloo, and Clabeck, four miles south of Halle. A narrow river winds along the valley, and across it, there is a railroad track. There are bridges at Braine le Chateau, Wauthier, and Sart le Moulin which are to be watched and blown up by our armored cars.

With patience and calm, as if he were explaining peacetime maneuvers, the Colonel shows to each of us in turn the new positions on his map. Three Messerschmitt fighters, followed by three light bombers, bring our peaceful palaver to a sudden end as they dive on our little wood. Picking up the maps, we rush headlong into the underbrush and scramble for shelter. Machine-gun bullets whiz through the branches nicking large splinters of bark from the trees. Our men have grabbed their Bren guns and return the fire. I am lying on my stomach behind the thickest tree I could find, wishing for the first time in my life that God had endowed me with the digging qualities of a mole.

The three bombers are over us now and the screeching of the bombs followed by deafening explosions sends the whole squadron sprawling flat on the ground. A few inches away from my face a fat teakettle boils on a petrol cooker as business-like and unconcerned as though it were setting on an *al fresco* picnic fire somewhere in England.

The German planes have gone on toward Halle. Only five bombs were dropped in our immediate neighborhood. They fell on the other side of our wood, one hundred yards away from where we are lying and near the spot where a few minutes before we were sitting with the Colonel.

The men are having tea. Some of them are singing "South of the Border," accompanied by one of the troopers who is an expert on the mouth organ. The Colonel before leaving stands silently for a while watching them. His face is drawn with fatigue and, as his gaze rests for a moment on the face of each man of our squadron in turn, it is as if he were trying to impress them in his memory. Many of them might be missing tomorrow.

As he walks slowly back to his car, talking to Andrew, the men stop their singing and, as if some mysterious order had been given, all of them, without a single exception, spontaneously snap to attention and salute his departing figure.

20.00 hrs. My orders are to go forward at once with Bruce's troop in Sgt. Ditton's armored car. I am to proceed to the bridge at Braine le Chateau and stay there, as this is the point where we are the most likely to make contact with French troops.

Peter's troop will be on our left; Tim will be in an armored car on the western end of Braine le Chateau and young Andrew will patrol the heights over Sart le Moulin. H.Q. troop with the Major and John will be at the crossroads to Lembeek on the heights between Braine and Halle.

We move off immediately. I am in the car which leads the entire squadron and keep my eyes on the map. At Sart le Moulin I turn right. The narrow river which borders the left side of the road is steeply embanked and I notice rows of field guns in position on the other side. Some are firing. We soon reach Braine. I jump out of the car and walk to the bridge, which is about two hundred yards up a road to the left. This road rises steeply beyond the bridge and leads to Hau-Ittre and Nivelles. It is paved and so is the bridge. The engineers who are accompanying me, after looking it over, say that it will take at least two hours' work to prepare the bridge, if they are to blow it up properly. They run to their small light lorry to fetch tools and explosives.

As I sit with feet dangling over the stone parapet waiting for I know not what, I catch sight of a long line of French soldiers coming toward me down the road from Nivelles. There are hundreds of them and they pass over the bridge slowly towards the rear. They belong to a North Algerian division, colonial infantry. They seem tired and demoralized and, after awhile, I notice with surprise that there are no officers with them. One of the sergeants asks me if they are on the right road to Lembeek. Some of them are wounded and some are in a state of funk. I inquire where their officers are but can't get much definite information out of them. About all I can learn is that they have been separated from their regiments; that their officers are dead or prisoners; that they ran out of ammunition; that dive bombers cut them to pieces and destroyed their mortars and antitank weapons; that the Germans are following close behind them; that a great battle has been lost, etc. They are mostly Algerians or Tunisians and speak French badly, but they are not deserters for a sergeant, who seems to be the highest in rank among them, has taken command. He tells me that the remnants of the division have orders to reassemble near Lembeek where he hopes they will be given food and ammunition to enable them to fight again.

It is getting darker. The engineers are pulling up the blocks of the paving and digging up the bridge. The Major arrives in the staff car. He has seen the French soldiers retreating on the road and didn't like the looks of it. I give him the information I have gathered. He tells me to stay where I am, but to have the bridge blown up as soon as I think things are getting too hot. He then starts towards Sart le Comte to inspect the positions of the other troops.

Sgt. Smith of the Royal Engineers who has been attached to our regiment, tells me that he will be ready to blow the bridge soon. The Nivelles road is empty now; the last stragglers from the retreating French division have all passed over the bridge more than twenty minutes ago. Night has fallen. Bruce has sent an armored car to protect us. It halts fifty yards short of the bridge, turns around and stays under the trees with its guns trained on the bridge. Its dark grayish mass, its clumsy and familiar silhouette are a comforting sight. I can always run to it if things start getting rough.

A dispatch rider brings me a message from Bruce. Orders are to challenge all loitering civilians and arrest, or even shoot them, if they resist or act in a suspicious manner.

Soon I hear the sound of a motor on the Nivelles road, and after a few moments I can distinguish a low dark car speeding down the hill straight towards us showing no headlights. The engineers jump under the bridge. I leap behind a tree. Sgt. Ditton fires two warning shots. With a loud screeching of brakes, the car skids to a stop just short of the bridge. To my relief, I see a French officer jump out of it.

I run toward him and recognize Lt. Lechatellier, a liaison officer of the French Military Mission. He seems surprised to see me standing here on this lonely spot and hastens to tell me that the

Germans are at his heels, having occupied Hat-Ittre two miles from here. Two French artillery officers are in the car with him. I tell him of my amazement at having seen hundreds of stragglers from the colonial division pass over the bridge heading for Lembeek without officers to command them. They remain silent for a moment without answering; then a French captain, his pent-up emotions finding an outlet at last, tells me of the terrible rout which he has just witnessed. His eyes are full of tears as he explains how the field guns have had to be abandoned through lack of ammunition.

"I went myself, three times today, to fetch shells for the guns at the appointed place," he says. "The dumps were empty, Monsieur. Three times I went there with my trucks and the dumps were empty!"

Lechatellier adds, "We have been badly beaten today. Everything was disorganized by enemy dive-bombers. It was horrible! The North African troops were completely surprised and demoralized by the German dive-bombers. And there was never an Allied plane in the sky to oppose them!"

He asks me what I am going to do here. I answer, pointing to the massive hulk of steel hidden under the trees: "I am here with the 12th Lancers who will try their best to slow the Boches down for awhile. More troops will be coming up soon and, God willing, we will stop them." This seems to cheer them somewhat. "Good luck, Messieurs," are the last words I hear as the French staff car speeds off on the road to Halle.

Another dispatch rider from Bruce. Two suspicious-looking civilians have been arrested by some of his men and he wants me to look them over and question them. Climbing up on back of the motorcycle, I go there at once. One man is obviously all right, his papers are in order. He lives in the village and had ventured out of his house to fetch his cows from a nearby field. I tell him to forget about his cows for the present and to go back to his house and stay there.

The other man, Flemish, doesn't speak French. I ask him for his *carte d'identité* and notice that his address is in a town north of Brussels. He has no business to be here, and I tell him to move on. He is rude and sullen. Poking my pistol against his ribs, I finally manage to get him off by pushing him, rather roughly I admit, toward the road to Halle and telling him in German to get out of the village or he will be a dead man. Flemish is very like German and he seems to understand. He walks away unwillingly at first, but after a few moments his pace quickens. I see him pass the last house of the village and disappear in the right direction. I climb back into the motorcycle and return to my vigil by the bridge.

A reddish glow lights up the entire horizon to the east and southeast. From Waterloo to Charleroi the Belgian countryside is ablaze once again. The same villages which have been soaked with French, British, and German blood twice in a little over a century are aflame for the third time. The same nations are once more tearing at each other's throats and shedding the blood of their children on exactly the same battlefield. It is a depressing thought.

Every now and then an explosion booms in the distance, flaring up in the cloudy skies and throwing a bright and vivid flash which illuminates the trees on the road ahead of me. Suddenly I hear the sound of motorcycles coming from Haut-Ittre. I run to the armored car and ask Sgt. Ditton to hand me a rifle and some ammunition. By the time I am back on the bridge, the noise has become much louder and is increasing every second. The engineers have stopped working and are listening. I tell them to get under cover and, placing myself behind the end of the stone parapet, I wait with my rifle ready for action.

Judging by the sound, the motorcycles are now only a few hundred yards away. Our armored car opens fire, pouring a stream of bullets over my head into the dark road ahead.

A moment later I see short orange flashes spurt from the right and left side of the road and several German bullets whiz over me. One nicks a stone on the parapet behind which I am crouching, while I hear others spatter against the steel side of the armored car. I believe that there are only two motorcycles with sidecars as two tommyguns are firing at us. Taking careful aim at the flashes, I fire four rounds at them and the engineer sergeant's pistol cracks several times from behind the other parapet. All this action makes quite a lot of noise; and the enemy patrol, probably believing that the bridge is heavily guarded, turns tail and flies back toward Hat-Ittre after shooting up a flare. The whole affair lasts only a few minutes, but there is no hesitating now; the bridge must be destroyed at once before Jerry comes back with reinforcements.

23.30 hrs. The ever-present and untiring Major, who has heard the noise, arrives in the staff car. I report the happening and he agrees that no time should be lost in blowing up the bridge. The dynamite charge is exploded to the accompaniment of a deafening roar which tells the Germans, who can certainly hear it from where they are, that one more bridge across their path has been made useless.

We soon discover that unfortunately only half of the structure has been destroyed and there is enough room left for infantry or even for motorcyclists to get across. But it is too late to do anything about it. After a word with Bruce, Andrew decides to take me with him as he thinks I may be more useful at his C.P. which is a good mile away on top of the hill between here and Halle.

EIGHTH DAY

Friday, May 17th.

THE NEW DAY is only a few minutes along when we reach the armored cars of H.Q. Troop about two hundred yards from the top of the hill on the counterslope toward Eshenbeek. The fighting lorry and the staff car are hidden on the extreme side of the road against the walls of a farm and turned toward Halle. The armored car in which John is talking to the Colonel over the wireless is under a slender tree in a track leading toward the Sart Wood. Andrew's armored car is a little further away on a cart road behind a short hedge. The third car of the troop has been sent to reinforce Bruce in Braine le Chateau as there are three small bridges to guard there in addition to the larger one where I was an hour ago.

Andrew is not at all satisfied with our present position as we do not have a commanding view over the valley; if an enemy patrol succeeded in getting through at Braine, it could be on top of us before we could do anything about it. Furthermore, the night is pitch dark. The stars and the moon are hidden by thick clouds making visibility very poor. So he decides to send me to the top of the hill with a party of men on foot. I take Machin, the driver of the staff car and three other men from our reserve in the fighting lorry, a Boys antitank rifle and a Bren gun.

We dig two shallow emplacements for the guns on the right and left of the road, then I sit in the thick grass on the side of the ditch, light my pipe and wait. This hill rises about three hundred feet above Braine and the valley toward Clabeck. From our position we command the road ahead and have a clear field of at least three hundred yards, yet we are practically invisible; we could, if need be, put quite a few of the enemy out of action and give time to the troops back of us to get into fighting formation.

After awhile the sound of machine-gun fire reaches us. It seems to come from Peter's troop to the left of the valley. Far away in the distance the sky is still red and I can see at times small lights flickering on the opposite ridge.

One hour later, I get orders from the Major to move forward a quarter of a mile down the road to a group of houses on the crossroads to Lembeek and to Sart Wood. The armored cars of H.Q. Troop, the staff car and the fighting lorry follow shortly after. Our new position is just half a mile short of Braine and at midpoint of the hill. It is a much better site as it affords shelter, concealment for the armored cars and two roads for retreat.

Some of the farmhouses are still occupied by their owners. My duty is to warn them to remain inside whatever happens, and I go from one house to the other banging on their doors and giving them this order. In the last farm, I find the door open and walk in.

All is pitch dark inside except for a streak of pale light under a door at the end of a hall. I push it open and enter a small room. In the semi-darkness a rather attractive-looking girl jumps out of bed with a scream when she sees me. She is in such a fright that she does not seem to notice that she is half-naked. She runs to a crib, which I hadn't noticed, in the corner of the room and picks up a wee baby who starts to cry. I apologize for my intrusion and tell her not to be afraid. When I say she must remain in her house, she begs me to let her leave with her small child and her old father, and putting the screaming baby on the bed, she even goes so far as to fall on her knees in front of me. As she clings to my hand, I notice that she is so beside herself with fear that she is trembling all over like a frightened animal. Only her hair, which is long, dark and rather beautiful, hides her bosom. Her nightgown has fallen off her shoulder—a fact of which she seems completely unaware.

I try my best to calm her, but this isn't easy with the baby howling on one side, and the rattle of machine guns on the other. I ask her where her father is and she tells me between her sobs that she has fixed a room for him in the cellar so he will be safe from the bombs. So I tell her to put some chothes on and I proceed to the cellar to have a talk with the old man.

He is a semi-invalid and is very sensible about his present plight, agreeing that there is no possible chance to escape now. When the girl finally comes down, sobbing quietly, with her baby at her breast, we both convince her that she must remain. As I take my leave, the grateful old man tells me that I will find a pail of fresh warm milk in the cowshed and that I may take it along. I walk into the warmth of the shed where I see three cows lying in the sweet-smelling straw peacefully chewing their cuds. I find the milk and carry it to the armored cars where Andrew, John, and the men receive it with joy. I drink two bowls of it myself and it makes me feel warm and comfortable. Our last sandwich was eaten over twelve hours ago.

2.30 hrs. John receives over the wireless the welcome news that a company of infantry and an antitank company are being sent up from Halle to reinforce us. No. II Troop reports that they have been under fire and consequently have had to change their positions slightly. No. I troop reports that they can hear motors on the hill beyond the river and see flashes, but that no attempt has yet been made to get near the bridges.

A formation of enemy bombers, flying very low, soar over us heading for Halle. Their shadows black-out the stars. A few minutes later we hear the distant thuds of their bombs exploding. Our reinforcements must be getting a taste of them. More bombers thunder by a few hundred feet over us; they too are going to Halle. Andrew thinks they will try to destroy the bridges over the Charleroi-Brussels canal, our only line of retreat. He decides to send me across the canal with the staff car and the fighting lorry. I am to find a sheltered spot on the Halle-Edingen road and wait there for further orders. This highway runs roughly parallel to our positions, but on the western side of the canal.

I leave at once in the staff car, followed by the lorry and two dispatch riders. Our first job is to get through the streets of Halle, which is still being bombed. As we reach the neighborhood of the bridge, we see several houses burning fiercely and about to crumble. There is a great deal of wreckage in the streets; some are entirely blocked. Happily, luck seems to be with us and there is a lull in the bombardment while we zigzag through the obstacles and get across the town. My driver is nervous and stalls the car twice, which makes me nervous, too.

We see quite a number of British soldiers about. They are all marching in a single file toward the bridge, keeping against the walls and in small sections.

We finally reach the Edingen highway which we follow for about two miles. Then we drive the cars to the side of the road under some thick trees and halt. I give the map reference of our position to one of the D.R.'s and send him back to the Major. It is about 3.15 and the night is very chilly. There is no traffic on the road and the only sounds which reach us are the low rumblings of cannonading in the distance between Mons and Charleroi. I curl up in the back of the staff car and decide to imitate Machin and the driver who are already snoring in the front seat.

I am awakened by young Andrew who has come to look for me in his armored car. I feel much better after my hour of sleep. Day is breaking and as I get out of the staff car to talk to him I notice the dead bodies of two Belgian motorcyclist soldiers lying on the road near their machine about thirty feet ahead and to the left of the road. They are riddled with bullets and, since I didn't see them when we stopped here, they must have been machine-gunned by an enemy plane while we were sleeping. Young Andrew is pallid from lack of rest, but cheery as he conveys to me the message from the Major.

"Things are getting lively down by the river and the Major is lonesome without you," he says smiling.

The Major wants the fighting lorry and the R.E.'s lorry which had come with Andrew to stay here and wait for further orders. As I do not think it would be healthy for them to be left here on the side of the road in broad daylight, I drive a mile up the road and find a good hiding place for the trucks under the trees of an orchard.

We visit a nearby farmhouse which has been hit squarely by a bomb. Bloody garments and baby clothes are scattered all about the place. At the back of the house is a pigsty. It has been hit, too, and a large sow is lying in it, dead and half-decapitated. Between her sprawled legs eight little pigs are squealing and pushing and poking their pointed pink noses into their mother's side trying in vain to suckle.

A few hundred yards up the road we catch sight of an abandoned black sedan of American make. Its front axle is broken so we decide to salvage its batteries for the Major's armored car which needs a new set badly.

Young Andrew's armored car starts off towards Halle, and I follow him in the staff car with Machin, who insists on coming along, and the driver. As we reach the bottom of the hill and turn into the main street of Halle, we can see more clearly than the night before the effect of the bombing attacks. The houses to the right and left have been turned into heaps of rubble and the streets and sidewalks are obstructed by wreckage of all kinds and descriptions. Some houses are still smoldering. Just as we come to the street which leads to the bridge I see three Heinkel light bombers streaking towards the town from the east. The armored car forges ahead and I urge my driver to follow at fifty yards and not to stop for anything.

Just then the first bombs come screeching down all around the bridge, which is about two hundred yards ahead of us, splashing up tall geysers of muddy water from the Canal. If we can get across before the bombers have time to wheel around and come back for the next attack, we are safe. At 50 miles an hour, through the black smoke and the dust raised by the high explosives, our wheels bouncing over the fallen bricks and timber, we follow the armored car in a mad dash toward and over the bridge—and we make it! The Canal is at least three hundred yards rack of us and we are practically up the hill and out of Halle when, through the rear window, I see the bombers launch their second attack on the bridge. In the car no one has said a word. Now, as I look at Machin and the driver, I notice that they are deathly pale. I know that I must be, too.

Andrew has moved his C.P. back and I find H.Q. Troop's armored cars in a deserted farmyard on the left of the road on the far side of the village of Eschenbeek. The set of batteries which we brought with us is much appreciated and is immediately installed in the forward link armored car, the wireless of which was getting faint.

The Major explains to me that British infantry and an antitank company, which have come up during the night, are holding the heights above Braine. The front line is about a half mile away at the spot where I left Andrew a few hours ago. Our armored cars are on the hill with the infantry.

A ruddy-faced Lieutenant Colonel who commands the antitanks has established his C.P. in the farm with us. His staff seems much disturbed over the enemy aircraft which keeps on thundering by only a few hundred feet over our heads. Some of the planes fly so low that they threaten to crash into the roofs of the farm buildings under the shadows of which we are crouching.

A young antitank subaltern timidly suggests that perhaps our pilots are still at bed at this early hour.

"Don't blame the b————s," grunts his colonel. "But from the look of things around here, I think they lie abed all day."

Everyone is beginning to feel uneasy and even mortified about the unexpected and total absence of British or French planes. Since the start of the German offensive, enemy aircraft have had the sky all to themselves. This makes it easy for them to fly in perfect formation and stunt over our heads as if in a peacetime airshow. They have been practically unmolested. Furthermore, Allied anti-aircraft batteries are conspicuous by their absence. Where they are, no one knows, but one thing is certain: they are not protecting us. The effect is far from happy!

I hear that the Guards have lost Louvain, and that the famous Dyle position, which was supposed to break up the German advance, has collapsed. The enemy, pushing forward vigorously on the heels of the retreating British forces on our left, is in the suburbs of Brussels. On our right the panzer divisions have reached Soignies and are progressing toward Edingen. Looking at the map, I can see that our small force before Halle is in great danger of being cut off from the rear. I glance up at Andrew and he, reading my thought, smiles sadly and silently nods his head. One thing is certain: If they succeed in destroying the bridge back of us, we are caught like rats in a trap.

It may be peculiarly a Frenchman's point of view that an empty stomach always has a bad effect on a man's morale, but when I suggest food to the Major, his weary face brightens and he confides to me that if I can succeed in digging up some kind of a breakfast he will see that I am rewarded with a V.C. at least.

I take Machin along and we both start on an egg hunt through the hayloft. We soon find two dozen eggs, and fifteen minutes later I am able to offer a large cup of boiling tea and a hot egg sandwich to all the officers and men in the farmyard. The antitank gunners are very grateful and thank Andrew and me profusely.

Without speaking, we chew our sandwiches and sip our tea, sitting on a low wall which surrounds the manure pile and, as the warmth in our stomachs starts to permeate through our bodies, we are able to look up with much less concern at the Junkers which are still droning overhead and diving at the bridge at Halle.

A dispatch rider arrives from Bruce's troop with a message for me to come at once to help him with a wounded French soldier who has just stumbled into their outpost. I jump in the staff car and drive up the hill. Leaving the vehicle at the infantry company H.Q., I walk over the crest with some forebodings as it is in full view of the enemy. Then, in a shallow ditch, I follow it to the small farmhouse behind which one of Bruce's armored cars is hidden.

The Frenchman is lying against the wall. Bruce, who is leaning over him, straightens up at my approach. "I am sorry, Henry," he murmurs, "it is too late."

I look at the blood-caked uniform and the gray face of the dead man and notice from his collar tabs that he belonged to a colonial regiment. I take his identification disk and papers, write his name and number on a piece of paper and place this in an empty bottle which has been found in the house. A shallow grave is dug and the body placed in it. I put the bottle in the grave. Bare-headed, we say a silent prayer, then we fill the hole with earth. All this is done very rapidly because we are being sniped at. After the little ceremony is over, we run back to the shelter of the wall and, with shaky hands, light cigarets.

Bruce appears extremely tired; he has had no sleep nor food since yesterday. As we smoke in silence for awhile, I look at his unshaven face, so covered with dust that his eyelashes are white, the puffed lids over his weary and bloodshot eyes and his soiled uniform. I can hardly believe that this is the same Bruce I used to know, rosy-cheeked, bright-eyed, and immaculate.

After a bit, he says, "I want to show you something. Something happened last night— something terrible—and I think you ought to know about it." He leads the way around the house and down the road which runs to the bridge at Braine.

"Watch out, sir," warns the sergeant as we pass by the foremost armored car. "I can see plenty of them b———— b————s hopping in and out of the bushes on the river banks."

Tight-lipped, without bending an inch of his six feet, Bruce walks on as if he has neither heard nor cared. At the bend of the road, a hundred yards farther on, I see a military car lying turned over on its side in the ditch. Bruce stops short and, with a nod and a look, asks me to go see what is inside. It is a French staff car, a Citroen.

I notice then that there is a large bullet hole in the center of the windshield just opposite the spot where the driver's head should be. Looking inside the car, I see the body of a French artillery officer. His head has been literally exploded by the bullet from Bruce's Boys gun, his helmet is crushed, his brains spattered over the upholstery. I suddenly feel very hot and uncomfortable and I can't utter a sound. Taking a deep breath I turn around and face Bruce. He is sitting in the ditch now, watching me. I can see how upset he is. I go and sit beside him and we stay there without speaking.

After awhile all I can find to say is, "Well, it wasn't your fault. No one could know it wasn't a Boche." Then, as he doesn't answer, I add, feeling that I must say something more: "Anyway, the man who fired that shot was a good marksman. My poor countryman certainly never knew what hit him."

We walk back to the farm and ten minutes later I rejoin Andrew and John at Eschenbeek. There I am told that the enemy has reached the Waterloo-Brussels main highway, occupied Sart le Comte, and that Peter's troop has fallen back.

Andrew lends me his binoculars and I climb up a ladder from where I can see the dust raised by the German armored cars on the road to St. Genese, the very same road we drove down on our way here last night. Then, as the deep detonations of antitank guns firing at the enemy reach my ears, I direct my gaze toward the edge of the Sart Wood and perceive rows of flashes clearly visible there.

Young Andrew and Peter's armored cars are now on the height on our left and are engaging the enemy. We can clearly hear their machine guns and every now and again the sharp crack of a Boys rifle.

A D.R., coming from our regimental headquarters, swings his motorcycle into the farmyard. He brings new orders; the infantry which are holding the line with us are to start retiring immediately behind the Halle Canal; they will withdraw one platoon at a time and dribble down the road toward the bridge.

This will take quite some time and Andrew calculates that two hours will elapse before the move is completed. The antitanks are to stay with us until noon, after which we will be left to our resources again. There is nothing else for us to do now, but wait and hope for the best.

While Andrew and the artillery colonel discuss the possible merits, shortcomings, and danger of this retreat in broad daylight, along a single road offering no shelter, toward the one and only bridge that remains open, John and I sit alongside his armored car. The sun is hot and we are both dead tired; we just sit there sucking our pipes, staring at the flies buzzing over the manure pile and enjoying the momentary peace.

Our meditations are abruptly cut short by a swarm of Junkers which come roaring straight down the road in threes, their machine guns blazing. We run for shelter as they zoom over us and a few moments later the ground rocks under the pounding of a rain of bombs crashing around our bridge at Halle. For a quarter of an hour or more they come and go at will, some flying in wide circles over the bridge, others in line roaring straight up and down our road machine-gunning incessantly. They must have spotted our retiring infantry.

Bruce phones that bombs have fallen in his vicinity, but reports no casualties. He says that the infantry have started to withdraw and he thinks some of them must have been caught by the blast of bullets and bombs. They are filtering back across the fields and through the hedges. Some are walking down in the ditches on both sides of the road.

Soon the first platoon passes our front gate. Many soldiers are wounded. They all seem very tired. Their leader, a young subaltern, waves at us. I run out and talk to him. He obviously is happy to be going away from here, if only temporarily.

11.00 hrs. One by one, the infantry platoons have filed past the gate of our farm on their way to Halle. The sun is blazing hot, and I am soaked in sweat and terribly fagged. We have been bombed twice, but neither the road near us nor the farm buildings proper have been hit. This continuous bombing is getting on my nerves and I decide to go into the orchard and sit for awhile in the shade of a large woodpile, alone.

I have slept about a half hour, pumped some cold water over my head and neck and feel refreshed and relaxed. Returning to the farmyard, I find the artillery Colonel giving orders for the withdrawal of his antitank guns at noon.

The Major and John are standing near the armored cars. They look glum. They have their earphones on and are listening to the report from our troops. Peter and young Andrew are doing very well on the left, although one car has been hit and two men have been wounded. As for Bruce and Tim, they report that they have fired at enemy patrols which have succeeded in filtering into Braine. Also that an enemy armored vehicle, either a light tank or an armored car, which came half-way down the hill leading to Braine and, seeing that the bridge was half-blown up and not wide enough, or being afraid that it might conceal a buried land-mine, backed up and disappeared over the crest.

From all this, it appears that, for the moment at least, only infantry threatens the Braine-Halle road on which we are, and that our worst danger lies on our left. There, Peter's troop must try to keep the German mechanized forces off the dirt road which would lead them to the Halle Canal and eventually, if they turned south after reaching it, to the bridge itself, thus cutting us off.

The antitanks are withdrawing. Their Colonel and his officers bid us farewell and good luck and leave for Halle. We are alone now. An ominous and extraordinary silence has suddenly fallen over the countryside. It is hard to believe that even at this moment crack German troops are crawling silently through the woods toward the crest of the hill. No firing reaches us. Overhead no planes are in sight, only the cloudless sky and merciless heat of the sun.

A half hour later, our Colonel calls up about the Halle bridge, just to remind Andrew that it is the only one left; he warns us to make sure that no anxious R.E. blows it up thinking there are no more Allied troops remaining on this side of the Canal.

"All right, Colonel," says Andrews, "I'll send Henry to investigate and tell them about us."

Three minutes later I am in the staff car speeding toward the Canal. The roadbed is torn up and we have to drive carefully to avoid huge craters and debris of all kinds.

The bridge has taken on a very warlike aspect since I saw it early this morning, but it is still standing. By some strange freak of luck, the bomb seems to have hit everything around, but left it unscathed. To the right and left, the Canal waters are filled with sunken barges. All the houses in the neighborhood on both banks have caved in under the blasts of high explosives.

On the other side of the Canal, the small square across the bridge has been hastily fortified. Machine-gun nests, made of sandbags and large paving stones, have been erected and through a hole in the only remaining wall of an *estaminet* an antitank gun points its long, thin, black muzzle. Dozens of British soldiers are hurrying about, bringing sandbags and stones to reinforce the positions, digging more pits, and carrying ammunition boxes.

Around the bridge itself R.E.'s are busy laying land-mines. The central part of the bridge has been torn up in several places and the holes are full of dynamite. All that is required now to blow it skyhigh is for someone to push a small button.

Leaving the car in a concealed spot a short distance from the Canal, I walk over the bridge looking for the officer in charge. The men all glance up sharply as I step cautiously around the mines. My uniform and French tank corps helmet, which is different from the infantry helmet to which they are accustomed, make me a stranger. I show my credentials and identity card and deliver my message, explaining to the officers who have gathered around me that our squadron is still holding the line of hills east of the Canal and that the only pressure we have had so far is from enemy tanks or armored cars on our left. We look at our maps and see that there is a bridge at Huinzingen, a mile north of here. When, and if, the German columns reach it and find that it is destroyed, they will have the choice of either turning left and trying this bridge or going north over the one at Lot.

They all seem grateful for this information and, when I leave them, it is with the promise that they will not blow the bridge until every one of us has crossed over. Just as I am about to return to the car, I see Edouard, my French colleague at Regimental Headquarters, coming towards me. He has been sent here by our Colonel to make doubly sure that the bridge will be kept open. It is a joy to see him and it cheers me up a lot. Everybody in the regiment loves Edouard. He speaks excellent English except for his pronunciation of certain words, and he has never quite lost the French way of saying "ze" for "the."

I ask him how he likes the war so far and he replies in English, "I zink it is a great sport, but I do not like ze bullets. Zay make a funny noise when they wheessle."

A quarter of an hour later, I am back at Squadron Headquarters and make my report to Andrew.

The minutes seem awfully long now that we are waiting for the order to withdraw. Standing here in the hot sun, in this messy farmyard by the manure pile and its buzzing flies, we all feel uneasy and restless. Even John, usually so calm, is beginning to show signs of strain. I think it is the ominous silence which surrounds us that causes this more than anything else. No sound reaches us from the hill, not a single shot is fired. The Germans must be moving up through the Sart wood between No. I and No. II Troops, unseen by them. There is nothing we can do about it. Armored cars are meant to fight on roads, not in woods. We must remain here and obey orders. Our squadron will stay on the hill and mount guard—a hopeless guard, since the ground is not to be held by the British troops—no matter what happens, until the order to retire is given.

14.15 hrs. The Major pulls off his earphones with a jerk and tells us to get ready to leave; the order has come through at last. I am to lead off in the staff car and collect the fighting lorry and the R.E. light truck which I have left this morning in the orchard on the Halle-Edingen road. Then I am to join the squadron at a rendezvous point north of Brucom one mile west of the Canal.

I push off at once and drive to Halle and over the now-familiar bridge as fast as the state of the road permits. I see Edouard still standing where I left him awhile ago near a machine-gun nest on the tiny square beyond the bridge. Without stopping the car, I lean out of the window and yell to him that the squadron is following behind me, and should be here shortly. He waves back to indicate that he has understood. As I look out of the rear window to catch a final glimpse of the condemned bridge, I can see his tall figure leaning against the sandbags with nonchalance appropriate to a thirsty lounger at the Ritz bar.

Avoiding the main street, which is strewn with ugly obstacles, we skirt the town, reach the road to Edingen, and find the orchard in which I left the two lorries earlier today. The men have made good use of a quiet morning. Blissfully unaware of the enemy advance, they have washed, shaved, and made minor repairs on the vehicles. But when I show them on my map that the German tanks are barely a mile away, quick action follows and fifteen minutes later all the cars are on the road heading back to Halle.

As we reach the top of the hill overlooking the small town, we hear, then see, the Stukas. They circle twice quite slowly, then suddenly one after the other they dart into a screeching dive over the eastern part of the town, which, after a series of earsplitting explosions, is wrapped in a sheet of flame.

However, we have to keep on driving straight toward this inferno. It would be self-murder to halt on the road now: they would be after us like hawks and there is no cover in sight. Black smoke and blaze are rising everywhere over the city below us.

Pulling out my map, as the car speeds ahead, I try anxiously to find a secondary road which might lead us to Brukom without going through the mess directly ahead. Just as we are entering the bombed area, a huge tree crashes a few hundred feet away and I see a narrow sunken cart track on the left side of the road. We swing into it at top speed. It has deep ruts and is tough going at first. I am worried for fear it will end in the fields, but luck is with us as we forge ahead and, by following one bad road after another, we manage to circle around the burning town. It takes us more than an hour to reach the crossroad near Brukom and there I find a D.R. waiting for us. He tells me that the squadron has gone by and the Major is expecting me at St. Kwintens.

The last twenty-four hours have brought vast changes to this little city. Most of the inhabitants have fled, hastily closing up their homes and shops. The cafés are locked; the little house on the square, where we billeted yesterday, is shut. There is nothing for us to do but sit on the edge of the sidewalk, spent and in a daze and watch long lines of swanky civilian cars speeding west filled with wealthy Bruxellois and overladen with luggage. A driver stops to ask me the way to Edingen and tells me that the Germans are expected to enter the capital tonight. This is terrible news, and hunger, thirst and despair are my only companions as I sit here on the pavement gazing blankly into space.

The Major has gone off to Regimental Headquarters to get orders. Bruce, Peter and Tim, sitting on the sidewalk with their backs to a wall, are sound asleep, their heads drooping on their chests. It is very hot in this dusty square. My body feels numb and lifeless. I, too, close my eyes.

The touch of a hand on my shoulder rouses me with a start. It is Andrew, back from Headquarters. He tells me to jump into the staff car and go to Herne, a village eight miles south of here, to prepare the billets for the squadron for the night. I feel empty-headed after my five minutes snooze in the sun and it is an effort to get up and walk to the car without stumbling over the rough pavement.

19.00 hrs. I arrive at Herne. It is a large village straddling the Ninove-Alost highway, about two miles north of Edingen and eight miles west of Halle. Here again, I am faced with empty and locked-up houses and, as I walk through the deserted streets, I feel discouraged at the realization that I must somehow find under these inhospitable roofs lodgings for the troops, covered spaces for the armored cars and trucks, a mess for the officers, etc. There is nothing for me to do but to get on with it. So, climbing over backs walls and smashing windows, I succeed in opening up a few of the abandoned houses and by the time the squadron arrives I have room ready for almost everyone.

An hour later, the tired and hungry men of Squadron A are in their billets and the vehicles are safely hidden in barns, sheds, or in orchards. Our quarters are in the lodgings of a caretaker of deserted brewery; two armored cars of H.Q. Troop, the staff car, and their weary crews share it with us. It is quite dark by the time everyone in the squadron is properly settled and I feel ready to drop when I drag my tired feet into the small dining room which, with two rooms above it and a small kitchen, make up our billet. On the table there is a half-empty whiskey bottle; the young subalterns are in convention around it, some on chairs, others on the floor. John is snoring in the only armchair.

Through the open door I can see the Major in the adjoining kitchen standing naked between two pails of warm water taking what he calls his "before-dinner bath." Machin is scrubbing his back while he keeps one eye on the stove where canned sausages, canned soup and canned potatoes are simmering.

The young lieutenants, who are silently sipping the whiskey, are fighting to keep their eyes open. Peter calls me to his side on the floor and hands me a bottle of wine which he has found in a house and kept for my special benefit. The good, heavy Burgundy revives me a little and enables me to stay awake until dinner.

When the tasteless food later is brought to the table, we force it down our throats in silence. We are much too tired to talk and, anyway, what would be the use of giving voice to our thoughts?

Only one thing is important, to try and keep as fit as possible, like a prizefighter who has but a minute's rest between rounds and who during that space saves his breath and recuperates his strength for the next round.

The arrival of a dispatch rider from Headquarters breaks the silence. He brings us orders to get whatever rest we can and be ready to move off at any time after midnight. It is now 21.30 hrs. With luck, we may manage two and one-half hours' sleep. We scramble upstairs and lie down on the bare floor of an unfurnished room. There are five of us on the hard boards side by side. In the next room the Major and John are sharing the only mattress.

NINTH DAY

Saturday, May 18th, 1.10 hours.

THE SOUND OF voices in the next room wakes me, and I recognize the Colonel's voice. I look at my watch; it is ten minutes past one. I have had a little over three hours' sleep. It is pitch dark outside, but a new day will dawn soon. A new day that means for us only German tanks, German planes, German bombs, the rattling of machine guns, blood and still more blood! All this rushes through my mind as I stare at the dark window, but I am still so sleepy that I really don't care what happens today, nor, even if I live to find out, where we shall be tonight.

I stumble down the narrow stairs and plunge my head into a cold-water bucket. Machin is in the kitchen heating water for tea. I am well awake by now and, after buckling my belt and strapping on my revolver, I go up to the room where the Major and the other officers are listening to the Colonel. The situation as I hear it is not pretty.

The Colonel briefly tells us that Brussels has fallen to the enemy —so have Halle and Soignies further south. The B.E.F. is not going to attempt to hold the Germans on this line. Our regiment, however, is to stay here to try and delay the enemy while the infantry retreats to an intermediary position ten miles to the west to make a stand back of the Dendre River. We are again called upon to fight a rear-guard action.

As I look at the Colonel while he talks, I wonder how he manages to appear so fresh, when I know that during every minute

85

of the day he is in constant touch with all his squadrons, personally directing their every move, and that at night, while we snatch a few hours' rest, he remains at his task, visiting each squadron, looking over the officers and men and pepping them up with always the right word of cheer and encouragement. The more I see of him the more I realize what a great leader he really is. I feel that I would do with complete confidence anything he commanded and I know that every man in the regiment would do the same.

3.30 hrs. The Colonel leaves. The armored cars file out through the dark and silent streets of Herne. We are heading east, toward Halle and the enemy. The countryside is covered with a low fog, heavy dew is falling; everything is cold and damp. I can hear no sound other than that of the squadron's motors and I find that I rather enjoy the peculiar sensation of driving blind through the fog and darkness, not knowing what is ahead and whether menacing sudden death in the shape of a German tank may not loom up in our path at any moment.

We have been on our way for one hour, moving ahead cautiously, proceeding and halting at intervals, and sending patrols forward. At dawn the squadron stops just outside a small village about five miles east of Herne. We are on high ground and I can see emerging from the fog the tree-tops of what looks like a large forest lying to the south between here and Edingen. Checking on my map, I identify it as the Bois du Strihoux.

Standing near his armored car, the Major gives out his orders to the troop leaders. They are to spread fanwise to cover a five-mile front between Pepingen on the Halle-Ninove road and Saintes on the Halle-Edingen highway. H.Q. Troop will move to a position near Bogarden at the center of the squadron's line. According to what we know, the enemy is to the west, south, and southeast of us.

Fifteen minutes later comes the order to mount and Bruce, Tim, Peter and young Andrew moved off with their troops, H.Q.'s armored cars, the staff car, and the fighting lorry follow shortly after.

5.15 hrs. We have just pulled up alongside a large farmhouse on the right side of a dirt road which runs through the hamlet of

Den-Dail. Already a company of light infantry is established here. Their most advanced post lies across the road about one hundred yards ahead of where we are. On the right, just beyond the farm building, is a field of growing wheat occupied by a platoon of machine-gunners. They are lying on their bellies with their sights on the crest of the hill between here and Halle. To the left, an anti-tank gun is hidden behind a low wall. These men have been here all night and we are to relieve them.

The few houses which make up the hamlet of Den-Dail lie on the highest part of an elongated hill which affords a commanding view towards the east and the south. At the corner of the cross-roads a few yards ahead of where I am sitting is a signpost marked on one side "Pepingen—3 km. 800," on the other "Saintes—3 km. 200." We are in the center of the squadron's battlefront.

Everything is strangely quiet here and the sky is filled only with the glorious rays of the rising sun burning slowly through the fog, veils of which are still lingering over the lowlands.

7.00 hrs. One by one, the infantry platoons have silently moved out of the village. They have left so quietly that I have barely noticed their departure and it is only when I miss them that the Major tells me that they have gone. It has taken just a little above an hour to complete the move and now our small group and its two armored cars are the sole occupants of the deserted village.

Eternally true to their British tradition, the men have made tea, Machin has found some eggs and we share a light and hurried breakfast, sitting on the ground in the shadow of the farm buildings.

Inside the stables, the starving cattle are bellowing. The cows have not been milked for at least two days, their udders are distended and the poor animals are wild with pain. As we have nothing to do for the moment, we untie them and chase them out of the stables into a grassy meadow where they can find food and water.

A lone observation plane is circling high above us now. This should indicate, since they usually work in cooperation with German armored units, that the Panzers are moving forward. I don't think the Boche sitting in this Henschel can see us, though, as we have done a good job of camouflaging the cars with straws and branches. The other vehicles are well hidden and there is no sign of military activity in the village.

Peter reports that he sees German tanks moving along the Halle-Edingen highway. That is where I was yesterday afternoon. Bruce reports that he has opened fire on enemy vehicles coming up from Halle on the Ninove road. Ten minutes later, he radios again to say that the vehicles have disappeared. At the same time, coming from nowhere and flying so low that it seems as if they were going to cut off the tops of the trees, three light bombers roar over us at a terrific speed. As they flash by, I can clearly see the bombs under their wings. They pull up sharply over the last houses and disappear towards the west.

We have now been here five hours and the warm sun added to the monotonous drone of the various German planes that fly above us makes me drowsy. We just sit and smoke and wait for something which isn't in a hurry to happen. It does not look as if the Germans are at all likely to want to come over this particular spot, and my own idea is that they are getting around us to the south.

Peter's troop reports that German armored vehicles are streaming steadily down the highway from Halle to Edingen. Bruce also sees plenty of them on the Ninove road heading northwest, but none are coming straight at us.

11.00 hrs. A message from Bruce. He is attacked by three light tanks. We can clearly hear the shooting coming from our left. The whip-like cracks of his Boys anti-tank guns sound above the clatter of the machine guns. We listen anxiously. Then, he reports he has knocked one tank out of action and the two others have turned tail. A few minutes later he speaks again; he has gone to the destroyed tank and found its three occupants dead.

Peter and young Andrew start calling, too. They say that the whole countryside ahead of them is swarming with German tanks, armored cars and motorcycle scouts moving toward their positions. While the Major and John are busy talking to them, and reporting in turn to our Colonel, the line of hills just opposite me is mantled with clouds of dust. Dark shapes are visible moving along the crest. As if they were conscious of impending danger, the cattle in the surrounding fields start to bellow and their plaintive cries mingle with the crackle of machine-gun fire, which is now being directed toward us from across the narrow valley. The Major waves us all back to the cars while reporting this to the Colonel.

By noon, several men have been wounded and a sergeant killed. One car is badly damaged. The Colonel orders withdrawal to Galmarden, a village east of the Edingen-Ninove road and six miles this side of the Dendre River. Each troop leader is to withdraw as he sees fit toward the Galmarden rendezvous.

The staff car, to which I have been assigned today, is hidden from the enemy by a high wall. Getting out, I stand on a large stone and peer over it. I can see four German tanks moving down the road toward the valley which separates us. They are out of range of our antitank rifles, but their machine guns keep pumping ineffectual bullets into our village.

As we see that some minutes will elapse before we get started, Machin and I decide that it might be appropriate to leave a welcoming committee for the invaders. So we go to the stables, where we had seen a large and mean-dispositioned bull tied up in a pen. We let him loose. He snorts and rushes on to the road while we jump into the staff car and speed off behind the first armored car as it swings left into a sunken dirt road which should lead us away from this village, unseen by the enemy.

We have been driving across fields and on cart tracks raising thick clouds of dust which I feel must be visible for miles. Just as I am worrying about what a wonderful target we must make, I hear a steady roar of bomber engines above our heads. I don't dare look up as I know too well what is about to happen. I decide instead to start filling my pipe to keep me busy and divert my thoughts. The brakes slam. A bright orange flame blinds me and a number of earsplitting explosions lift the car, knocking me into the dashboard. Acrid smoke and clouds of dust choke me for a few seconds. I leap out of the car as if impelled by a spring. The armored car, which was ten yards ahead of us, is on its side in a deep gully. Andrew comes running up and calmly orders all hands to get busy and try to pull the car out of its perilous position.

For five minutes, we dig and push while another armored car skids and tugs at its bogged-down mate. Just as we are about to succeed, and the car is on the verge of being righted, its driver makes a wrong move and it falls back into a deeper hole. Our work is made more difficult by the constant attention that two bombers are showering on us in the shape of short bursts of machine-gun bullets which streak through the dust alarmingly close by. My shirt and tunic are soaked with sweat from heat and fright. Nothing short of a miracle can now lift the armored car out of the hole which its spinning wheels are digging ever deeper and deeper as the motor races in a desperate effort to wrench the heavy hulk out of its impending grave. Andrew, who has worked twice as hard as any of us, finally straightens up and reluctantly calls the whole thing off. All equipment and weapons are removed and the Major himself ends the life of the armored car with his own pistol, shooting the engine full of holes.

We move on across the sun-baked and dusty plateau, reach the Ninove road at Herne, and over winding country roads, arrive at Galmarden.

Our sudden appearance frightens away two suspicious-looking civilians who are very busy looting a brewery. In their flight they abandon in the middle of the road a large wheelbarrow filled with bottles of beer. This is too good a piece of luck to pass up, so I jump out of the car, move the wheelbarrow out of the way and come back with the bottles which I distribute to our thirsty crews, keeping a few for the troop leaders and myself.

Outside the village, parked under the tall shady trees lining the Moerbeke road, we find Bruce's and Peter's troops waiting for us. One of the armored cars has a large antitank bullet hole in it. We sit around in the tall grass along the bank of the road and are busy enjoying my beer treasure trove when young Andrew's crew joins us.

We can't help laughing at Andrew's appearance when he scrambles out of his armored car. None of us is clean, but he beats us all; his hair and eyebrows are so covered with white chalky dust and his eyes so lined with black wrinkles that he looks as if he has been made up to play the part of an old man in a school Shakespearian play.

The Major, who has been busy on the radio-telephone ever since we arrived, collects us around him in the ditch and gives us the new positions we are to hold, which he has just received from the Colonel. The squadron is to spread out in a rough semi-circular six-mile line stretching between Vane at the northern end to a point south of the Bois de Lessines near the Edingen-Ath highway. We have to get across the Edingen-Gerardsbergen road before the enemy reaches it. There is no time to lose for according to the latest information the Germans have already gone through Edingen and are hard on our heels.

We have just crossed over the road and are already being shot at from all angles. The Major calls me to his car and asks me to take the staff car and the fighting lorry out of the way a bit west of the Lessines Wood. He sends an armored car to accompany me.

We halt under some thick trees at the northwestern corner of the wood and I report my position to squadron H.Q.

We are well-concealed under thick foliage when at least twenty bombers roar over, barely skimming the treetops, and a few minutes later I hear the crashing of their bombs about two miles to the west in the Dendre valley. They must be after the Lessines bridge. The sound of steady and heavy firing comes from the south where the German tanks and motorcycle troops are attempting to reach Lessines by the main road which joins the Edingen highway at Ghislenghien.

Peter and his troop are watching it from the north while a squadron of the East Riding Yorkshire Yeomanry straddles it a mile east of Ghislenghien. This cavalry unit is motorized and equipped with light tanks. Their French liaison officer is my friend Philippe de Croisset; he is patrolling the road in an armored Bren gun carrier and, after sending me his greetings through Peter, hurries on toward the village of Silly, south of the highway where most of the shooting is taking place.

Three antitank guns are sent up from Ath to help the cavalry tanks and our armored cars. Unfortunately, they set up their position back of us and fire at the British tanks, mistaking them for German. Three of the light tanks of the Yorkshire Yeomanry are blasted by them and their occupants killed before they can be stopped. They are ordered back to Ath.

During all this the large black bombers have kept up the plastering of Lessines. Dozens of them in an unending stream fly over our wood on their way to the small town through which the squadron will have to pass shortly, if the Germans leave the bridge intact. Black smoke and hot ashes blown over us by the westerly wind make the sky gray and hide the sun.

The pressure on our squadron is getting worse; the enemy is attacking from all sides and our troops are hard-pressed. The crossroads at Ghislenghien is now in German hands and enemy motorcyclists, followed by tanks, are moving on toward Ollignies and Lessines to cut us off from the rear. Our squadron has lost contact with the Yorkshire Yeomanry light tank squadron who are retreating toward Ath and putting up a stiff resistance.

The Major directs me to go to Deux-Acren, two miles north of Lessines and make sure of the bridge there. His orders are that the squadron shall stay on this side of the river until 20.00 hrs. if possible, then to retreat over the bridge.

15.00 hrs. I have just crossed the railroad track and the bridge over the Dendre River west of the deserted, wrecked and still-smoking village of Deux-Acren. We are now on high ground and have a good view of the surrounding country. I can see the houses burning in Lessines and for a long distance to the north, over the valley of the Dendre

As I cannot leave the vehicles exposed on the main road, where it is impossible to conceal them, I post a motorcyclist to watch for the squadron and drive a few hundred yards down a farm road towards some barns under which we shelter the cars. There is nothing for me to do but to wait and, sitting on some straw, I examine the squadron's position on my map: they are practically surrounded and still have an hour to go. I am suddenly overcome with a great feeling of helplessness and anxiety for my companions and overwhelming fatigue.

I have been here just a little over an hour when I see a D.R. coming towards us. He has orders for me. The squadron is crossing the Dendre now and I am to go ahead immediately to Buissenal, about ten miles west of us, where we hope to get food and perhaps a few hours' sleep. Our day's job is over.

I indicate the position of the village on the map to the drivers and we leave at once, with long intervals between the cars, driving towards the dense black smoke which now covers the flaming town of Lessines which we must pass in order to reach the road to Buissenal.

We tear down the highway at full speed without stopping, skirting huge craters, dodging burning trucks, charred bodies and crumbling walls, and finally, after endless minutes, we reach the top of the hill west of the town and turn right into the small road heading for Buissenal.

Basil, who commands our transport echelon—with which we have not been in contact since we left St. Kwinten over two days ago—greets me at the entrance of the hamlet. He tells me that the town is already filled to overflowing with hundreds of frantic refugees and he has had a difficult time finding billets for the squadron, adding that the armored cars and transport lorries will have to spend the night under the trees of a large orchard. The only thing that I am really interested in is the fact that I won't have to run around and do the billeting, because I am so tired that I can hardly stand.

He leads me to a farmhouse where our cooks are busy preparing supper and advises me to rest a bit until the Major arrives with the troops. Standing in the courtyard as if in a dream, I see Bruce and his troop come roaring up the village road through the dusk, and the bleary-eyed, gray-faced, wornout crews stumble out of the armored cars.

I enter the noisy kitchen of the farmhouse, and Tich, our mess corporal, seeing the condition I am in, silently pushes a wooden stool under me. I flop down, close my eyes and fall asleep immediately.

The Major's voice giving orders to the squadron arouses me from my slumber. I look at my watch. I have slept ten minutes!

A small girl has just entered the kitchen. She has immense dark eyes, thick, curly, black hair and her skimpy pink dress is crumpled and soiled. She holds an infant in her arms and she begs for a little milk for the baby, her brother. I want to go back to sleep, but there is something so appealing in her quiet, assured,

older-than-her-age tone of voice that I can't help watching her.
Her right shoe is split open, her feet are swollen and sore and,
while the milk is being made warm, she sits up very straight on a
chair with the baby on her lap and tells me her story.

She has walked all the way from Brussels, forty miles, in a day
and a night. She is eleven years old. Her parents, German Jews,
used to live near Berlin, but they had to flee when the Nazis came
to power and settled in Brussels. Soon they found jobs and things
were beginning to look brighter. Then came the baby brother, the
war, and the invasion. Once more they fled. She tells me that her
mother and father are sick and that she has left them lying on some
straw in a barn nearby.

I can see that she has serenely taken upon her frail shoulders the
whole responsibility for the family. She wants nothing for herself,
only for her father, her mother, and the baby. Her only hope, her
goal, is the frontier of France. She seems to feel that if she can get
her family across the border they will be safe forever. She knows
that they have over thirty miles to go, but she is a most amazing
small person, in her absolute certainty that the Allied troops are
to stop the Germans—at least long enough for her to get to the
border. I do not contradict her.

She asks me if I think it will be safe for her to lie down and
rest for a few hours. "Because you see," she adds, "I am very tired,
and my feet are very sore."

I promise her that I won't let her oversleep and will wake her
up before we leave which will certainly be early in the morning.

The kind-hearted woman who owns the farm and who has
overheard our conversation brings some hot water in a basin to bathe
the child's feet and also gives her a pair of rubber sneakers to replace her worn-out shoes. Our cook makes sandwiches for her
and her family, and, as the brave child leaves the kitchen, she
thanks us with exquisite politeness and, with the dignity of a
queen, solemnly steps out into the dark night holding her tiny
baby brother in her tired, aching arms.

I follow her to the door and watch her as she crosses the courtyard and enters the straw-filled barn. As she walks away in the
night, she suddenly seems to grow in stature and embody the spirit

of her persecuted people as well as the undying determination of
the human race to live on. And I suddenly feel ashamed of my
weariness.

23.00 hrs. The armored cars have been refueled and their ammunition supplies replenished; the men have been fed, the wounded
attended to and in silence we have eaten our usual lukewarm
supper of canned soup, canned sausage, canned potatoes.

A radio operator brings us orders. We are to leave at 3.00 A.M.,
returning to the Dendre River to try to hold the heights above
Lessines while our infantry withdraws.

There isn't an unoccupied square foot of flooring anywhere in
the house on which to lie down and sleep; all the rooms are filled
with refugees. So I roll up in my blanket under a damp pile of hay
in the orchard.

TENTH DAY

Sunday, May 19th, 3.30 hrs.

THE NIGHT IS very dark and cold when Machin wakes me. Around me the crews of the armored cars are stirring, their black shadows moving in and out of the trees which are lighted up every once in a while with the flash of a torch. One after the other the motors are started up while, faithful to my promise, I go to the barn to wake up the little girl and her family, but they are already up and ready to trudge on, pushing ahead of them the baby's carriage overflowing with what they have been able to bring with them of their poor home treasures.

Thirty minutes later we too file out of Buissenal and the heavy armored cars move along through the darkness, heading for the ridge above the valley of the Dendre southwest of Lessines. Proceeding cautiously, and without lights, over dirt roads and bumpy tracks, we reach Ostiches just before dawn.

The 4/7 Dragoons' (light tanks) C.P. is already established there and our Major reports to their Colonel.

The quaint village is deserted, except by the owner of a cafe-general store on the main square near which we halt. The shopkeeper, a kindly and buxom woman, who has refused to follow the example of her fellow-townsmen and abandon her groceries, is busily serving coffee and giving away all that there is in her shop to anyone who wants it. She tells me to take anything I like and hands me a hot bowl of café-au-lait. She wants all her shelves and counters to be bare when the Germans arrive.

6.00 hrs. Our combat troops have left for their advance positions between Lessines and Papignies; the Dragoons' tanks are on their right flank from Papignies to Rebaix. H.Q. troop, with the two armored cars it has left, the fighting lorry, staff car, and four D.R.'s move out of Ostiches toward Wannebeck, a small village two miles east in the center of our position. The country lane on which we are driving is bumpy and dusty, so we proceed slowly, going and stopping by fits and starts. As we reach the hamlet of Enfer, "hell" in French, we get a report that two enemy tanks and some motorcycle troops have made a crossing at Lessines, which is two miles away. As if to confirm it, the sound of intense gunfire starts up suddenly in that direction.

We reach the center of Wannebeck and halt. The Major takes one armored car forward on reconnaissance to Lessines. The sun is very hot, so, leaving the remaining armored car on the side of the crossroad against a wall, we place the lorry and staff car in the shade of two large farm buildings and John and I sit on a doorstep, awaiting the squadron leader's return.

There are no enemy aircraft above us for the minute. Thank God, for they could spot us easily.

Antitank guns are banging away at the enemy all along the front. Unfortunately, we won't have them with us for long, as they are to withdraw shortly and we will have to stay here keeping watch until noon without their help.

7.30 hrs. The Major returns with good news. The two German tanks have been stopped cold and for the present all is well on our left flank. He decides to move us out from this village to higher ground and we leave through a small country lane which takes us to the crest of the hill a mile northward near Sart, where an isolated farm makes a very good C.P.

We are at the junction of road No. 60 leading east to Lessines (two miles) and a secondary road going south to Papignies (3 miles). There is plenty of straw about and the men camouflage the armored cars to make them look like strawricks; the lorry and the staff car are hidden under sheds.

We receive bad news from our right flank; the Dragoons are up against some heavier tanks near Rebaix. Our own Regimental

Headquarters telephones to confirm the Rebaix report; several German tanks have crossed the river there and the Dragoons are slowly falling back. We might be cut off if the enemy succeeds in getting his tanks north towards Ostiches and Lahamade on our rear. We have no more anti-tank guns with us, the last unit has just passed by going west.

10.00 hrs. We got news from the Dragoons; they are putting up a good fight, knocking out some of the heavier tanks, but others are now reported swarming up the road between Rebaix and Ath. The Major sends me down the Lessines road a few hundred yards to establish a post. I find a good position and place an antitank gun in the right ditch and a Bren gun in the left one. My gunners have a clear view of the road for nearly half a mile, and if any Jerry ventures before our sights, he will get a hot reception.

I have been sitting behind the Boys rifle for over an hour now. The sky is filled with light Heinkel bombers. At first they fly along the valley, wasting their high explosive bombs on the positions which the anti-tanks previously occupied, and each time they pass over Wannebeck they dive down and machine-gun its empty streets. Later, though it can't possibly see anything stirring on the road we are on, one of the bombers sweeps down on it, firing short bursts from its machine guns while we hug the muddy bottom of the ditches. The sound of cannonading which has died down in the valley ahead reaches us now with increasing intensity, not only from the south, but also from the southwest, and seems to get nearer every minute. I have an awful feeling that this time we are really surrounded.

12.00 hrs. We are ordered to retreat at once and we hurry back to the farm where we find the armored cars already moving out, shedding their straw coats as they go. The Major tells me to jump into John's armored car which is to close the rear of our column.

Keeping wide intervals between the cars, and at top speed, we tear down the road toward Lahamade, heading for the safety of the thick woods between that village and Buissenal. John tells me that the squadron's orders are to reach Frasnes if possible, probably to take up a position behind it and guard the Ghent-Valenciennes highway. Frasnes is ten miles southwest of here.

Our three troops are fighting their way out of the German pincers and fleeing towards the rendezvous by separate roads. As we approach Lahamade, two large bombers fly straight down the road over us and I clearly see two bombs tumble out of one and three from the other. The first two crash directly ahead near the ditch on the right side of the road, the other three explode in some farm buildings at the entrance of the village, blasting them to bits.

The Major's armored car, which is in the lead, thunders ahead, disappearing in the smoke and dust raised by the explosions. The lorry and staff car follow at top speed. We are two hundred yards behind them.

13.00 hrs. We have reached Frasnes, crossed it, and halted a mile and a half west of the Ghent highway. Our three troops are there ahead of us. The remains of the Dragoon regiment are drawn up under the tall trees on the left side of the road. They have been badly knocked about. Three of their Bren gun-carriers are loaded with the wounded and dying. I can't help wonder when and where these men will be attended to, as I haven't yet seen a British doctor or ambulance since the campaign began.

My friend, Bob, the French liaison officer with that squadron, is sitting, with his eyes closed, at the back of a small battered lorry with his dead British captain lying across his lap. I walk over to speak to him and he smiles wearily as he recognizes me. His breeches are soaked and stiff with blood and, as he asks me to light a cigarette for him, I notice that more blood is trickling down his right hand. He has been hit hard in the shoulder but doesn't seem to know it. I believe he is still suffering from shock and does not realize that his captain is dead. His only idea is that he must get him to a hospital.

Our squadron has been luckier and less exposed than they. We have had no major casualties and all our cars have returned, though some are badly scarred and have jagged, gaping holes in their armor plate.

Orders arrive for the remaining Dragoon tanks and our armored cars to start off at once to reconnoiter the roads leading south and southwest from Frasnes.

A thick black cloud of smoke rises far to the west, blocking out the whole sky over the city of Tournai. Hundreds of bombers are flying over it circling and diving. The heavy thuds of the explosions, which are flattening that lovely town only a few miles away, follow each other so closely that they sound like a barrage of big guns.

Several batteries of field artillery speed by us followed by divisional cavalry tanks who are all withdrawing behind the Escaut River. The two other squadrons of our regiment and Regimental Headquarters squadron also pass us going to the rear. The Major is warned that there is only one bridge left over the Escaut at Tournai and that the German bombers are trying to smash it. The road to Tournai is congested with traffic and I feel much safer standing here on the side of the road as I dread to think what will happen when the Luftwaffe starts going after the retreating columns. One hour goes by punctuated by the crash of explosions. Then I see the remainder of the Dragoons' tanks, who have also been ordered to withdraw, pass by us heading down the dangerous highway.

Once again our squadron will be the last to withdraw. Our troops are still courageously patrolling the high ground beyond the Ghent highway without help or hope of help from anyone.

The Major calls me over to his armored car and tells me that, as there is no sense in leaving the staff car and the fighting lorry here, he wants me to start at once with them and wait for him across the river on the heights beyond Tournai.

15.00 hrs. I shake hands with Andrew and John and, much as I hate to, I leave them. A dispatch rider is to come along with us and I tell the lorry driver to follow the staff car in which I am riding at a distance of one hundred yards.

The road is a mess. Huge trees blasted by bombs, burning trucks, wrecked cars and transport buses riddled with bullet-holes bar it at several points. The bodies of disembowled horses have been blown up on the embankments, and in several places men's bodies lie mangled and bloody in the dust. Straight ahead the smoke column rises ever blacker and thicker and bright red flames leap skyward over Tournai, mercilessly pounded by the savage attack of the Luftwaffe which goes on and on without a let-up as more and more bomb squadrons fly in to replace those that have emptied their bomb racks.

A few miles down the road in a nearby field I see hundreds of refugees who have been crowded off the road by the military traffic. Men and women are huddled together in pitiful groups with their hastily-gathered belongings piled high on carts beside them. The poor creatures have reached the end of their trek. They are hopelessly trapped now between the flames of Tournai and the fire of the murderous panzers.

As we speed by, I recognize with dismay in one of these groups the pink dress and tousled black hair of the little Jewish refugee girl from Brussels. At her side is the battered baby-carriage, now with a broken wheel. She clutches the baby in her arms, as she stands looking defiantly at the road. Poor kid! All her efforts and courage have been in vain. I want to wave to her, but something stops me. Perhaps it is the fact that she had seemed so confident last night that we would protect her. And here we are, fleeing westward, leaving her behind!

We have now entered the Tournai inferno and halted not far from the bridge. As far as my eyes can see, there is not a single house left standing. Down the river to my right the railway station is ablaze. All the streets leading to and from the bridge are blocked by crumbled houses. The last British light tanks are crossing over the bridge and some Royal Engineers are trying to clear up the heaviest debris to enable them to pass. There is going to be a wait, and I feel very uncomfortable sitting here in the staff car in the middle of the road with no protection whatsoever, and so near the bridge which is the target of the planes above.

The bombers have spotted the tanks and are swooping down. Now is the time for us to get out of the way, so my driver cleverly heads the staff car practically inside a blasted shop window. In this unorthodox position, it probably looks like a wrecked car, and the Germans ignore us. I then scramble out and yell to the lorry driver to back up a few hundred yards and get under cover until he gets my signal to go ahead.

The tanks now are across the bridge, climbing the narrow street on the other side. There is a lull in the bombing so I signal to the lorry; we put the staff car back into the road and make for the bridge through the path which the tanks have cleared.

As we reach the Grande Place where a few days ago I took leave of Cdt. M. on my way to Brussels, it is hard for me to believe that this is the same spot. The quaint houses are scorched and empty shells; huge blocks of cement, stones, bricks, steel girders, burning rafters, lie across our way. Only the cathedral, with its seven beautiful spires seems untouched, but the ancient and world-famous library filled with priceless medieval manuscripts which adjoins it is roaring with flames. Live wires from trolley cars lie twisted on the ground and at first it looks as though we would never be able to get across the square. Two women run through the debris screaming, desperately searching through the smoking wreckage while a little farther away an old man, his white hair caked with blood, stands before what was his home poking aimlessly with a stick at the remnants of a huge dining room table.

Jumping out of the cars, pulling the wires and pushing stones and slabs of cement out of the way, we succeed in getting out of this hell. We are all so shaken by the horror of what we are seeing, by the wanton cruelty of this destruction which is beyond belief, that no one says a word. Our faces are pale and grim; our eyes alone speak. For there is no spoken word which could adequately describe our feelings and the atrocity we are witnessing.

We halt just outside the town and wait for two hours for the squadron to arrive. A tremendous explosion tells us that the bridge has been destroyed and there is no point in waiting any longer. I still have hope that the squadron may have taken another road parallel to this one leading to Douai. We start off, taking a short cut through the fields, and reach it. There, to my great relief, I find a D.R. who tells me that the squadron has gone ahead in the direction of Orchies, in France.

17.00 hrs. We have just reached the French frontier. Long files of refugees so fill the main road that we make slow progress. I have a feeling of relief to be in France again. It is like entering the shelter of a harbor after having been tossed for days in a storm at sea. Here, for the first time since the offensive started, the air is filled with the robust booming of any considerable collective number of antiaircraft guns. German planes at long last have to keep high and they are closely followed by the black puffs of exploding shells. A battery of heavy French artillery, long 155's, rumbles up along the road heading in the right direction, east. A huge antitank ditch, camouflaged concrete pillboxes, miles of barbed wire, defend the terrain. There are evidences of military efficiency everywhere, in marked contrast to what we have seen and been through.

At Orchies, a D.R. from Regimental Headquarters is waiting at the crossroads and directs me to Thumeries, a small village south of the Phalempin woods where I find the rest of the squadron and our transport echelon already established in their billets.

There is a French antiaircraft battery in the rear of the villa in which we are housed. The gunners are a gay lot and prime marksmen. Every time they bring down a German plane they celebrate the kill with whoops of joy and sharing of liters of red wine. This, strangely enough, seems to improve their aim and I watch them shoot down three bombers in less than an hour. A heartening sight!

Orders and fresh news come from our Regimental Headquarters after dinner. We hear for the first time what the outside world has known for days: The Germans have broken through on the Meuse and at Sedan on May 17th, and a mechanized army, pouring through the gap, is heading for the Channel, having already by-passed Cambrai and Arras. Because of the danger from enemy parachutists, dressed as civilians, and Fifth Columnists and Communists who have attacked isolated officers and attempted sabotage in different places, there are strict orders that no officer or trooper is to go about alone or unarmed.

It is hard for me at first to realize the implications contained in this disastrous news, and it is only later on, as I lie sleepless on the hard mattress in the room which has been assigned to me, that I awake to its depressing significance.

ELEVENTH DAY

THE SQUADRON IS speeding down the road to Lens, towards Arras. I count sixty German bombers in the air on our left; they are swarming above Douai, repeating the same murderous tactics they used yesterday over Tournai. No aintiaircraft fire peppers the cloudless sky today. The guns have either been silenced or withdrawn, and a pillar of smoke a mile high ascends from the French city.

A column of artillery moving south and troop-carrying lorries moving north form a traffic jam just outside Lens. They are going to the front, but it looks as if the front were all around us now! We halt near a railway grade crossing waiting for the road to clear and, getting out of the car, I walk to the signalman's shack. A few hundred yards down the tracks on my right an enormous locomotive and its tender lie on their sides derailed. A railroad worker is sitting dejectedly on a bench outside the shack staring at them.

I ask him why nobody seems to be trying to clear the line. He answers with a shrug: "What the hell is the use? Les Boches have cut the line south of Arras. It is all up with us here!"

I feel the blood rush to my head and hear myself repeating after him stupidly, "Les Boches have cut the line . . . cut the line!"

Now I know why a new-born baby cries when the cord is cut. It must be a cry of despair because the link with the mother has been cut and he is cast off alone. Well, our cord has been severed.

105

The long, steel cord which joined us to the heart of France. I want just to sit here near my countryman on his bench and stare at these steel lines which I see for the first time for what they really are—life arteries . . . ! I never had paid much attention to them before, but now that they are lifeless, I want to go and touch them and feel their cold, substantial smoothness under my palms.

The command to mount takes me back to the car. I know it is no use trying to share my feelings with my British comrades because they wouldn't understand. A Britisher never believes he is cut off, so long as he has the sea behind him.

We pass by the huge Canadian war memorial at Vimy and turn right into a secondary road leading towards Mont St. Eloi. The nearby fields are filled with British soldiers belonging to the 5th and 50th divisions moving up to position around Arras. Two batteries of light field guns of the Royal Artillery are ready for action, standing in the center of the fields without shelter or camouflage. Ammunition lorries, staff cars, motorcyclists, speeding to and fro on this country road, raise high columns of dust. There seems to be no thought of concealment in anyone's mind. If we had acted this way on maneuvers there would have been hell to pay. Perhaps there will be, now.

We halt behind some of the guns and our Major jumps out of his armored car to talk to a staff officer who gives him very bad news. There appears to be doubt whether the elements of a Guard's battalion which, with a motley of other hastily-gathered units are inside Arras, are still in control there or if the Germans have entered the city, which is only four miles away. We also hear that General Weygand is in command instead of General Gamelin, about whom wild rumors circulate.

We move on and halt a little farther up the road in a shady spot where thick trees provide concealment from two Henschel observation planes which are circling above us and the batteries. Seven Somua tanks of the French 1st D.L.M. pass by, heading east. I stop one and talk to its commander. He tells me that they are off to make a counter-attack near Bailleul, about six miles from here and near the Lens-Arras highway, which we have just left.

We stay here till noon when we receive orders to feel our way around the west side of Arras and to find out what we can about the enemy's exact position and his strength between there and Doullens.

15.00 hrs. We have proceeded by short stretches and have crossed the highway leading from Arras to St. Pol. We are now four miles south of it and ten miles southwest of Arras on a winding country road leading to Avesnes. We halt beyond Hermanville because this narrow road is deeply embanked and the thick hedges surrounding it block our view.

The Major, John, and I get out and, taking rifles, climb to the crest of the hill along the left side of the road to see what is going on beyond it. Running across the fields, we reach the top and lie flat in the cool green clover from where we have a wonderful view of the main road leading from Avesnes to Arras. It seems full of what through our field glasses appear to be long lines of refugees with heavy carts flowing southwest. There is so much dust around them that it is difficult to distinguish whether there are any German tanks which have slipped in between the carts, as they often did. So, after observing a while longer, we run back to the cars and move forward.

The Major sends Sergeant Knight's armored car ahead to reconnoiter the entrance to Avesnes. We follow it. Suddenly the sound of shots down the road brings us to a halt. A few minutes later Knight's armored car returns. There is a large hole in the armor plate. They ran smack into an enemy tank half a mile from here and it opened fire on them before they had a chance to know what was happening. Corporal Chambers was killed and the Sergeant wounded in the neck, but the driver, with the greatest skill and calm, managed to back his car and turn it around in the narrow road while the Sergeant, without wasting a second, swung his guns toward the enemy tank and let him have it with his Boys gun. He thinks he stopped it dead. Anyway, it didn't fire again or move.

The Major is all for going after the tank right away, but just as he reports the incident to the Colonel we get orders to move back north of the St. Pol highway immediately, as the squadron on our left has reported that they see German tanks coming up the highway back of us heading toward Aubigny. They will cut us off unless we get there before them.

17.00 hrs. We have reached the highway, crossed it and gone through Aubigny without meeting opposition. We halt for awhile in the little village of Bethonsart in order to bury Corporal Chambers. Speedily the men dig a grave in a small field two hundred yards south of the church under the spreading branches of a large oak tree. This quiet pasture, surrounded by thick green hedges, is reminiscent of an English landscape. It is a fitting resting place for a soldier of Britain.

After standing in reverent silence for a few moments, we return to the cars and move off at once, reaching Frevillers at 18.00 hrs. This village, six miles east of St. Pol and two miles north of the Arras highway, stretches for about a mile on both sides of a country road running along the crest of a ridge. As we pass by the church, a group of French cavalry motorcyclists catch up with us, shouting that they have found one of our rear D.R.'s lying on the road badly wounded. The lorry is dispatched to pick him up.

Frevillers is already occupied by a squadron of the French 1st Cuirassiers, part of the 1st D.L.M. I get in touch immediately with their commanding officer, Cdt. Vignes and introduce him to the Major. We learn from him that his division has suffered staggering losses; they have fought hard and continually since May 11th and are now only a shadow of their former strength. Nearly 80% of their equipment has been destroyed and they have only about twelve Somua tanks and a few Panhard armored cars left, two of which are defending this village.

When the Cdt. sees our wounded men, he sends for his medical officer. The motorcyclist is too far gone to be helped much and he is immediately sent to a hospital in a French ambulance. As for Sergeant Knight and the other wounded men, they refuse to be evacuated after having their wounds dressed and, with typical British distrust of any foreign diagnosis, tear up the tags on which the medical officer has so painstakingly written a description of their wounds with a request that they should be x-rayed at once since they are certainly full of steel splinters.

Plans are drawn for the joint defense of the village by one of the forward troops, the two armored cars from H. Q. troop and the two Panhards of the Cuirassiers. Bruce's and Peter's troops take up positions south and west of the village on the heights overlooking the highway to watch the enemy and report his moves.

At nightfall I am sitting in a ditch back of a Panhard fifty yards away from the Major and John, who are talking by wireless to our Colonel and to our troop commanders. Everything is very quiet, though there is a deep rumble of artillery fire coming from the east beyond Arras. A French officer has just told me that there is a rumor that General Corap, who commanded the 9th Army on the Meuse, and General Gamelin have committed suicide. Though no one attaches much credence to these rumors, the French soldiers seem to think that these two generals are directly responsible for our present plight. They don't mince words about it.

At midnight we are ordered to proceed at once to Festubert near La Bassee where our transport echelon is waiting to give us some food and refuel the cars. This village is at least twenty miles away and I fear we will waste a great deal of time on the jammed roads trying to get there.

TWELFTH DAY

May 21st, 4.00 hrs.

WE HAVE NOT had quite two hours' sleep and we are driving back to the front line through the damp and chilly night. I hear that we are now part of a force under the command of General Franklyn, comprising parts of the 5th Div., the 50th Div., and the army tank brigade. We are returning to Frevilliers which we reach at sunrise.

The Cuirassiers are still in the village when we get there, but they tell us that they are expecting orders to leave shortly as their division is moving to strike east of Arras. The armored cars resume the positions they held last night and Bruce's and Peter's troop move away for reconnaissance towards St. Pol.

Even at this early hour, the sun is warm, and the exhausted Major, who hasn't had a minute's rest, has difficulty keeping his eyes open as he sits in the ditch at my side. I urge him to sleep awhile and I remain near him to see that he is not disturbed.

Colonel de Vernejoul of the 1st Cuirassiers drives into the village with three Panhards. I wake up the Major and introduce him. They immediately take to each other and get busy with their maps, exchanging much mutually needed information.

The French Colonel, who I can see is very much impressed by Andrew's bearing and fighting spirit, is keenly interested to know what our troops have found out about the situation around St. Pol, which he thinks is the danger spot. We show him on our maps the points where our armored cars have come into con-

111

tact with the enemy this morning. Peter, who is on the right above this city, has reported that it is so packed with refugee carts, which have poured into it from all directions, that no one can enter the town, or leave it for that matter. The enemy has found that out, too, and is now circling around it from the south. North of St. Pol, the Germans have not yet set foot on the Lillers road, which one of our troops has under constant observation.

The Colonel has gone and Cdt. Vignes invites Andrew, John and me to share breakfast with his officers in their improvised mess. The hot coffee, thick-sliced French army bread, and cold pork— I was told the young pig was grunting happily on the streets of Frevillers only yesterday morning—make a new man of me.

The stampede of refugees has now become a matter of life or death for us. They must not be allowed to go on blocking the roads and impeding our movements. Strict orders have arrived concerning them, and I spend the next few hours stopping carts which are attempting to go through the village. Twice I have to pull out my revolver and threaten the peasants to make them turn back. These unfortunate people are frantic. They have fled southwards to escape the invader and have bumped right into him again. Now they want to go back home and our orders are to stop them.

14.00 hrs. The Cuirassiers have reluctantly bid us goodbye and we are left alone in the village. Bruce reports that long lines of German trucks, tanks and armored cars are speeding down the highways leading west. They all carry bright orange strips of cloth spread over their radiators, probably so that their own planes will recognize them.

Young Andrew has run into trouble close to Bailleul near the St. Pol road: his forward armored car was put out of action and two of his men are wounded, but he has blasted the enemy tank which did the damage, killing the crew of three.

16.00 hrs. We are withdrawn and move to Mont St. Eloi, the scene of bloody battles during the first World War. The squadron is sheltered in an abandoned farm on a hill a mile west of the village and under the towering war memorial which rises above it.

Four miles southwest of us, the city of Arras, which has been for seven months the capital of the B.E.F., is agonizing, and the combined Franco-British are making a desperate attempt to relieve it. At this minute, a powerful striking force, consisting of an infantry regiment, the army tank brigade, with 58 medium and 16 heavier tanks, plus two batteries of the Royal Field Artillery with the support of the remaining tanks of the D.L.M.'s, are trying to break open a passage around south of the beleaguered city. They started off from the village of Mareuil, a mile south of Mont St. Eloi, two hours ago, and the latest reports place the west column about five miles south of their starting point. They are fighting their way into Warlus, a village five miles due east of Avesnes where Corporal Chambers was killed yesterday.

The Major assembles the squadron in the farmyard and tells us that if this afternoon's raid succeeds we are to push forward to-night right through the German-held territory to try and make contact with the French armies thirty miles south, who will also be attacking in our direction. He explains that, if our counter-attack is successful, the Boche panzer units between here and the sea will be left high and dry, cut off from their supplies. He ends with a smile, "Of course our regiment will be in the lead. We shall push forward as far as we can and, though we may be knocked out before we reach the other side, others back of us will carry on the good work and carve their way through."

Every single man in the squadron standing rigidly at attention in this courtyard knows what this order means. They know that our armored cars have armor only one-third of an inch thick; that our armament is totally inadequate, and that we will be massacred at the first road block we meet. We might as well ride forth tonight on horseback. At least there then would be a reckless glamour to the adventure.

After the order to dismiss is given, the men salute smartly and with magnificent discipline silently go about their work: refueling, greasing, replenishing ammunition and cleaning the guns. The sound of a fierce cannonade reaches us from Arras and also from the Scarpe River valley east of it, which is held by a crack battalion—the Dragoons of the French 2nd D.L.M.

After watching the men for a moment, the Major and I walk

away together and enter the lower room of the farmhouse where we find two comfortable, though broken, chairs. We flop down in them and, lighting up, smoke in silence, pretending to relax— each trying to hide from the other the nervous strain against which we are fighting. I feel instinctively that something is gnawing at him inside, something quite apart from our present military situation and I wonder what it is and if I can help. Being French, I speak first, tell him my personal worries, give him the address of my mother and ask him to do certain things in case he comes back and I do not. Andrew listens kindly to me and then hesitatingly tells me what is on his mind. When the offensive started he was anxiously expecting to receive news about the birth of his child but, like all the rest of us, he has had no word from home since we went into battle. He has no way of knowing how his wife is or whether the child has been born— and now he wonders if he will even live to see it.

"By God, I will make you the godfather if we come back, Henry," he says. And for a few minutes he relaxes. He puts his arm around my shoulder and tells me that he does not think that I should go forth with the squadron tonight as he can't put me in an armored car, anyway, because we are short of them, and I would have to tag along in the staff car, which would be suicide.

I don't know what to answer. All of a sudden I feel terribly tired emotionally and incapable of thought. Just at that moment he is asked to report at Regimental Headquarters.

18.30 hrs. The whole area between Vimy, Mont St. Eloi and Arras is under attack from the Luftwaffe. I count more than sixty light bombers and twenty-four fighters in the air showering bombs and machine-gunning. The earth rocks under incessant explosions and the atmosphere vibrates with the roaring of their motors, the screeching of the tumbling bombs and the metallic chatter of machine-gun fire. Their attack seems to concentrate especially on the area around Duisans, two miles south of us near the Arras-St. Pol highway.

We all get under cover and Machin, who has found a way to the cellar of the farm, calls to me to join him there. When I reach the bottom of the steps, I find him beaming and surrounded with twelve bottles of very excellent Pomard. Since it would be a crime to allow them to be smashed by bombs, or even eventually drunk by the enemy, I distribute them. We may need them tonight.

An hour later the cars are ready, the men are having tea, and Peter, Bruce, young Andrew, Tim and I have a magnificent meal of biscuits, bully beef out of the can, and Pomard out of the bottle.

The bombing has not stopped, but has shifted eastwards, letting up in our immediate neighborhood a bit. We have been lucky so far, none of the farm buildings has been hit, though some bombs have fallen pretty close by. The only casualties have been some cows in the nearby fields.

We are waiting for orders and the Major's return and are trying not to think too much.

21.00 hrs. The Major arrives and immediately gives orders to assemble the squadron. Everyone stands at attention. He tells us casually that the attack which was to have taken place tonight has been called off by the High Command, and that we are to move immediately to Grunay, a suburb of Lens, where we will spend the night.

This is an anti-climax after what we had been led to expect we were in for. I watch the faces of the officers and men as they listen to the Major's words. They are all intensely pale. I think that I also see the eyes of some filled with tears, but to a casual observer only the tenseness of their jaw muscles would have betrayed their emotional stress under the let-down.

The Major then explains to me that the raid made this afternoon by the tank brigade has failed to reach its objectives and that this force has suffered considerable losses, including the Commander of one of the tank battalions. Though, at first, they did succeed in crossing the Doullens highway, they were not able to get much farther as they encountered strong antitank resistance which they could not overcome.

As night falls, the squadron moves down the hill toward Vimy and Lens. I am in the armored car which is in the lead, reading the map and looking for short cuts. As we enter Bully and are about to cross the railroad tracks which separate this town from Grunay, several shots are fired at my armored car and at the staff car following behind us in which John is sitting. The bullets miss us. They came from the windows of a large factory on the left side of the road. Its gates are wide open and, after a moment of stupefication at having been fired on by apparently my own countrymen, I tell the driver to go ahead and drive into the factory courtyard and circle it.

We halt at the front door of the administration building. Two civilians, who say they are caretakers, run out and ask us if we have heard shots. I tell them, "We damn well have, and I am here to find out where they came from." Their excitement and perturbation seem genuine. One of them tells me that the factory is empty, but that some of the workers, whom he calls Communists, might have slipped in, though he can't imagine why they would do such a thing. I suggest it may have been parachutists who have been dropped in the neighborhood, but the caretaker seems doubtful.

There is no point in staying here all night and arguing. We have neither the time nor the patience to search the buildings, so I warn the two men to lock the gates behind us when we leave and tell them that they will be held responsible if any other incidents of the kind occur again.

At Grunay, we have to resort to strong-armed methods and axes to force our way in through locked gates and knock down front doors to find shelter for the men and the armored cars. All the houses are closed up and abandoned; their owners have fled.

After a hasty dinner, John, Peter and I lie down on the floor of the dining room of the small villa which we are occupying and get a few hours' sleep.

THIRTEENTH DAY

Wednesday, May 22nd

UP AT DAWN. No orders yet, so we shave and have some tea. There is a radio set in the house and we listen to the news from Paris:

"Amiens and Abbyville have fallen to the Germans," but the commentator blithely adds the usual line, "The situation is well in hand. The Allied air forces are taking a severe toll of German planes. Important reinforcements are being sent to the front . . ." etc. etc.

It would be funny if it wasn't so tragic. It is like getting news from another world, yet Paris is only a hundred and fifty miles away. But how and when shall we get back to it—or shall we ever?

8.00 hrs. The squadron leaves for Neuville St. Vaast, two miles southwest of Vimy. There we find Squadron B waiting for orders and I have the great pleasure of running into my colleague Pierre Linn, who is its French liaison officer. I haven't seen him since the blitz started and there is plenty to talk about. He has heard that the Germans have fought their way into sections of Arras and that some of our friends, including Captain Dick Furness of the "Guards," was killed during the action.

Our general situation is certainly not improving. The Scarpe river line is held east of Arras by the French and west of that town up to Mont St. Eloi by British infantry. From there on there is a wide undefended gap into which the Germans are pouring tank forces which are pushing northwards in an attempt to isolate and annihilate us.   Our job will probably be to ride forth into the gap and find out just how far the Boches are getting.

From Neuville we drive up the hill to Mont St. Eloi and halt near the farm where we spent yesterday afternoon.   Our Colonel is waiting for us.   He tells me the depressing news that our friend Edouard, who was his French liaison officer, is reported missing after going on a reconnaissance west of Arras and is believed to be either dead or captured.

The Colonel sends the squadron off to reconnoiter the heights northwest of Villers au Bois along the Houdain-Arras road.   It is in the valley below this ridge that a strong enemy force is attempting to push northwards across the Scarpe river between Acq, Capelle-Fermont and Villers-Chatel in an effort to turn our Vimy and Lorette positions from the west.

We reach Villers au Bois, go through it and into a small country lane which, according to the Major's British map, should lead us to Camblain.   It is not marked on my French map, however, and this puzzles and worries me.

After about a mile, the road peters out into a mere track through the open fields with no trees for shelter.   Our cars are raising clouds of dust which are certainly visible for miles as we are driving over high ground.   Our marching order is: The Major's armored car, the staff car, John's armored car, the fighting lorry, Sgt. Knight's armored car, and the three motorcycle D.R.'s.

I am in the staff car trying to figure out on my map just where this track will lead us, when I hear the roaring of aircraft motors and see with dismay small puffs of dust raised by a stream of bullets hitting the middle of the road ahead of us.   I yank the door open, and, looking up, see three Messerschmitt fighters sweeping down on us from the north, hedge-hopping at about one hundred feet.

They flash by over our heads like streaks of blue-gray steel and they are immediately followed by three more which I can see are diving straight for us.   There are two large strawricks about one hundred yards ahead on our right, and I shout to the driver to head into the one fartherest way, so that the lorry behind me may

take cover under the other. We hit the straw with a bang and
pop out of the car like corks from a bottle of champagne. Twenty
yards away the men in the lorry do the same.

Meanwhile, the armored cars and the D.R.'s have passed us
and speed on, cutting across the fields from the south, heading
for a curtain of trees three hundred yards away.

The German fighter planes make a sharp rising turn and now
come back at us with all their guns blazing. From where I lie on
the ground I can see the first armored car reach the trees; the
second and third follow at wide intervals, their machine guns
spitting away for all they're worth at the German planes. All
around me white puffs mark the impact of the German bullets as
they streak through the dust. The two rear D.R.'s are shot off
their motorcycles, hit the ground and crumple up, but the third man
spurts onward and manages to get under the cover of the trees.
The aerial carrousel has changed its aspect now: the enemy aircraft have formed an immense wheel in the air over us, zooming
up and diving down with machine guns crackling.

One of the Messerschmitts flies straight at me and I hug the
rough soil for dear life while I feel and hear the steel bullets
stabbing into the ground around me. When I finally look up
again, I can see no sign of the armored cars, though I can hear
Bren guns and also what sounds like antitank guns banging away
just beyond the trees behind which the squadron disappeared.
For ten more minutes the Messerschmitts let us have it, then,
just as suddenly as they came, they decide to leave us alone, wheel
off to the left and disappear.

My knees feel like rubber when I get back into the car and
anxiously try to find on my map a way out of our cul-de-sac. The
two D.R.'s are only wounded and I send them back to our
Regimental G. P. near Mont St. Eloi.

I am terribly worried lest the other cars have gone on without
us, for the enemy is not a mile away and the slightest mistake
would drive us right into their lines. Furthermore, we have to
get back to some kind of a road as the staff car and lorry are not
built for this cross-country driving. The only possible chances
I can see of hitting a road are by advancing straight towards the

sound of the battle; returning to Villers au Bois—which I refuse to consider; or following the very distinctive tracks left in the field by the heavy tread of the armored car tires which we might be able to trail to wherever they have halted. I decide to adopt the third course and, bouncing over the deep furrows of the plowed fields, we proceed as cautiously as we can to avoid breaking springs or axles, and eventually reach the line of trees which I discover to be on a long wooded ledge immediately above the Scarpe river valley.

We push through the underbrush at a spot where it is not so thick and, to my great relief, I soon recognize the silhouette of two of our armored cars. Our arrival is hailed with joy by John and the crews when they find out that we are unhurt.

They have not fared so well. One of the cars has been put out of action, riddled by the armor-piercing bullets of the Messerschmitts. Sgt. Johnson has been killed and our C.O. was slightly wounded in the left hand while shouldering a Bren gun to return the enemy's fire. John tells me that Peter's troop has also had a sharp encounter with the enemy and Peter has been severely wounded. Six other men in the squadron have been wounded so far this morning, not counting our two D.R.'s.

The Major, who had gone off to reconnoiter toward Acq, returned and while the guns and equipment are being taken off the disabled car and it is being blown up, I use all my powers of persuasion to get Andrew to stand quiet long enough to have a bandage put around his bleeding hand. He seems to consider this wound a personal insult and it has acted on him like a spur to a horse.

We move off through the trees behind the two armored cars searching for an outlet. Shortly we reach a wider lane from which we can observe the valley below us. The enemy is crossing the Scarpe at Acq, a mile south of here, and we can see the flashes of antitank guns which are blasting away at the German armored vehicles, while an unceasing stream of machine-gun fire rips the valley as a greeting to the green-clad infantry which is crawling through the bushes.

Well hidden behind a wooded embankment, we see enemy

troops advancing on the two small roads which lead up to our ridge from Frevin and Acq. After watching for awhile, we ride towards the northwest and soon find ourselves once more driving over the open fields between Cambigneul and Gouy. Then we cross a railroad track, hit a country road, and speed on towards high trees which according to my map form the park of the chateau of "La Haie," which lies halfway between Gouy and Villers au Bois.

12.00 hrs. It is a relief to have our cars well hidden under the tall trees lining the driveway which leads to the chateau. The Major is busy speaking with the remaining troop leaders over the wireless telephone, and John tells me that I can get out and stretch my legs as we will probably stay here for a long while.

Walking away, I enter the abandoned cottage of the gatekeeper. The occupants must have fled from their home in precipitate haste, judging from the cold remains of an interrupted meal and a half-empty glass of red wine on the table, as well as the garments and linen which are strewn all around the room. As I walk into the next room which is in semi-darkness, the outside shutters having been closed, I am startled by two shining eyes staring at me in the dark, soon followed by a deep growl.

A brownish birddog lies curled up on the pillows of what must have been his master's bed. I talk to him but he won't move. He lies there looking at me with wide, feverish eyes, whining pitifully. I notice that his nose is dry and that the poor animal must be thirsty and ill. Machin, who has followed me in the house, fetches some water in a bowl and we put it on a chair touching the bed. Then we try to tempt the dog with some biscuits, but the wretched beast won't budge and keeps burying his nose in the pillows moaning. Deserted by his owners, but faithful to the end, he will remain here waiting for the return of his master—or until death overtakes him.

Fifteen minutes later, we are back in the cars moving off towards Villers au Bois, and, as we turn out of the park onto the road, we see two men running across the field waving at us and shouting. We halt. As they get nearer, we see that they are two men from Peter's troop. They are breathless and exhausted,

and tell us haltingly that their armored car was knocked out of
action, the third member of the crew killed, and that they barely
managed to escape under the very nose of the advancing enemy
by hopping from hedge to hedge until they reached a safe distance.   Then, trusting to luck and good sense, they headed northeast, hoping to encounter the remainder of their troop.   They are
lucky indeed to have found us in time because it certainly has
saved them from being captured.

This means we have lost one more car today, and this one with
its weapons, ammunition and all the crew's kits.

The Major tells the men to hop into the fighting lorry and we
move off again. We drive through Villers au Bois and on to
Carency.   There we hear that Peter's wireless operator has been
killed and Corporal Chorley, who has managed to disengage the
car with the greatest of skill, is driving his severely wounded
commander away from the battle and trying to locate a field hospital.   The other troops are hitting and dodging under the constant direction of the Major, who is in great form today and doesn't
miss a trick.

Some enemy patrols have been seen near Vimy to the east and
others were observed approaching Houdain to the northwest.

16.00 hrs. German light tanks and motorcycle scouts are entering Villers au Bois. The squadron has moved northwards and is
stretched out on the high ground along the Lorette heights.
Andrew calls me over and asks me to take the staff car and the
lorry at once to Festubert, a small village across the Aire Canal
half way between Bethune and La Bassee. He wants me to make
sure about the bridges over the Aire Canal and see about billets
for the men.

I leave at once, enter Souchez just after it has been bombed and
strafed by machine-gun fire, and turn north on the Bethune highway only to find it barred by the flames from two large gasoline
trucks which have just been hit. There is nothing left to do but
skirt around them and drive into the fields. This we do with
some apprehension, but our always dependable staff car and the
lorry take us through the ditches and the soft plowed furrows
swiftly and surely.

Back on the road, we make slow progress as the whole length of it is jammed by columns of trucks moving north. They are being incessantly attacked from the air. Finally we reach Cambrin after having had to bale out and hit the ditches several times; we cross the only bridge left over the Canal and arrive at Festubert. It has taken us nearly two hours to drive less than twenty miles!

I find Festubert already filled with French troops belonging to the Cavalry Corps of General Prioux. Our transport echelon is waiting there, too, and Basil tells me he has had a hard time finding empty space. After investigating thoroughly every house in the village, he has finally had to be content with four isolated houses situated about a quarter of a mile outside and north of the village.

When I come out of the café assigned to the officers' mess, I notice that eight French medium tanks have gathered in the open square around the church, probably because of faulty billeting arrangements. Anyway, retribution comes quickly in the shape of waves of Heinkel bombers which sweep down on the village, dropping high explosives, machine-gunning everything in sight and making everyone scurry for shelter like rabbits. I count more than twenty of these planes as I lie flat in a ditch half filled with filthy water. After ten full minutes in this undignified position, I am joined by Machin who is in search of a deeper hole. We wonder if this hell will ever come to an end and if they will ever let us relax a bit.

An hour later, H.Q. troop arrives and John tells me that they have had exciting moments since I left. Andrew, rash as usual, decided to ride ahead on a sunken country road to find out what was going on beyond the next hill. Just as he started up the winding lane a German light tank cleared the crest of the hill coming toward him. From where John's armored car was halted, he could see them both, but neither the Jerry nor Andrew could see each other. John decided to fire some shots at the enemy tank, although it was out of range, in order to attract Andrew's attention. Andrew, not knowing what all the shooting was about, ordered his car to duck behind the farm building half-way up the hill so he could investigate. The German tank, which was being shot at and apparently didn't like it, swung right and hid on the other side of the farmhouse. By now, Andrew, who had had a glimpse of the other tank, but who thought it might be a friendly one and was willing to give it the benefit of the doubt, jumped out of his armored car and, going to the corner of the building, waved the little Union Jack with which every car had been provided for just such circumstances. John tells me that there was only one thing for him to do then: to keep on firing ahead away from Andrew. The Major, deciding that after all something must be wrong, scrambled back into his car while the Jerry, bewildered, turned tail, got back on the road and drove away in a cloud of dust over the ridge to safety, pursued by volleys from both John's and Andrew's car.

Peter's armored car pulls up. The first thing I notice is that the little plush monkey mascot has fallen from the hood and is now a shapeless, torn mass hanging on the mudguard. Behind where it once sat so gayly, there is a hugh jagged hole. I don't want to go near the car nor do I want to be told what caused the dark brown stains inside the turret which I can see from where I stand. I welcome the excuse to walk away which is furnished by an excited old woman. She shows me a broken pair of earphones and a very primitive radio receiving set no larger than a cigar box which have apparently been found in her cellar. She has cause for worry for she has been told that the French troops on the other side of the village have issued an order to shoot on the spot anyone found with a wireless receiving set. As I don't think she looks like a spy, and everyone in the neighborhood tells me she has lived in the village for the last fifty years, I take her along to a French officer, who, after listening to her story, keeps the broken radio set and lets her go.

It is quite dark when the rest of the squadron arrives, and after a hasty meal we all lie down exhausted on the tile floor in the main room of the café where we are billeted. Through the broken shutters the glare which illuminates the sky to the west paints the ceiling above me ruddily and reminds me, as I lie sleepless and tossing, that six miles away Bethune is in flames and that somewhere among this mass of raging fire and crumbling ruins there is a hospital where my friend Peter lies dying. Last night he and

I shared the same mattress, and this morning as we started off he gave me his final tin of pipe tobacco, saying that he wouldn't need it any more....

A tremendous explosion rocks the earth coming from the direction of La Bassee. The last bridge over the Aire Canal has been blown up.

FOURTEENTH DAY

Thursday, May 23rd.

THE COLONEL IS HERE talking to Andrew. I look at my watch: it is three o'clock

Thirty minutes later the armored cars have been driven out of their sheds and are lined up in the pitch darkness along the village road, quiet except for the sound of their idling motors. The order to mount rings out, the car commanders scramble into the turrets, and one after another the cars move off toward Bethune and St. Omer.

The situation, as I have just heard it from the latest reports, is highly critical. The enveloping maneuver against our forces is progressing every hour. From our southernmost pivotal point up to the sea, the German tidal forces are lapping against Mont St. Eloi, the Lorette heights, Houdain, Bethune, Omer and Gravelines, eight miles west of Dunkirk. The already badly battered Franco-British troops now have to face the enemy not only to the east and south, but also to the west—with no reinforcements or relief in sight!

The squadron is speeding towards the Liller-Aire area west of the Canal D'Aire to the rescue of some columns of guns and trucks which are attempting to withdraw behind the protection of the canal before the German armored forces can stop them.

12.00 hrs. The squadron is now in a very exposed and dangerous position from which it might well be impossible to extricate itself. The imminence of the danger seems to have an exhilarat-

127

ing effect on Andrew who is patrolling about fearlessly in his armored car and taking delight in personally reconnoitering the most hazardous spots.

Two miles to the north Bruce and his troop are in a tight fix. He is screening the withdrawal of a long column of lorries and guns on the road to Hazebrouck. Four tanks are attacking him. By his clever and incessant maneuvering he succeeds in drawing away the tanks which otherwise would have fallen on the retreating column and destroyed it.

John and the Major go off on a short reconnaissance. John's car is in the lead. Several antitank guns firing at once crack sharply out of sight beyond the ridge ahead. They are followed by a few bursts of machine guns, and a few minutes later John's car returns with a large shell-hole right through it and his mangled body crumpled up in the bottom of the turret.

During all this, our Colonel, at his battle headquarters on the ridge on the western slope of the Mont St. Eloi ridge, is lying on the ground watching the enemy movements below and around him. They are so close that he can see them easily without field glasses. He warns the High Command and tells them that he can count more than forty-eight tanks coming up through Villers au Bois.

An hour has gone by and the situation is getting worse and worse. The German tanks, which the Colonel saw, have rolled over Mont St. Eloi, taken the Lorette heights and Souchez and are practically in the suburbs of the city of Lens. Nothing but the outmatched and outnumbered force, consisting of the few remaining tanks of the British tank brigade and some Somuas of the D.L.M., stands in their way.

I am ordered to proceed to Carnin, two miles north of Carvin and about four miles east of La Bassee.

Near Bethune a French Somua clanks up the road coming towards us from the Bois des Dames, and I notice a gaping hole just below its turret. It halts and its commander, a Sergeant of Cuirassiers, waves to me. He wants our help to carry out of the tank the headless corpse of the driver. When this is done, he and the other man of his crew take a big swig from their wine bottle; then, easing into the driver's seat behind the hole, he wheels the heavy machine around and they speed off toward the enemy to avenge the death of their pal.

We have been held up for more than a half hour by a traffic jam caused by the bombing of the crossroads ahead of us. Ammunition trucks are exploding and fire is spreading; there is a great deal of confusion. We get under shelter and wait until the bottleneck clears up.

This countryside is probably the least-suited in all France in which to fight, and I can see how easy it must be for the enemy to advance through the densely inhabited, but undefendable villages and suburbs of this mining district. Huge slag heaps, some over three hundred feet high, provide the Germans and their parachutists with ready-made O.P.'s from which they can command these flat lowlands and its net of highways.

As we are about to get on the Somua returns. Its sides and tracks are covered with dark bloody stains. I recognize the Sergeant and see that his face is beaming as he hails me. Yelling so as to be heard over his motor, he excitedly tells me that he was lucky enough to run right into a troop of enemy infantry near Barlin. Charging through them and slashing right and left, he had mowed them down and ground them under the tracks of his machine until there were none left in sight.

"My *copain* is avenged and now I must hurry back to my unit and a good bottle of wine," he says. We shake hands and he rumbles off.

16.00 hrs. At Carnin I find our transport echelon established inside a large farm and our cooks already busy in the rear of a grocery store, which they have found half-looted and which we board up again in order to save from the greedy natives the hundreds of food cans still on the shelves. Most of the houses are locked up and their shutters closed, but I soon discover that many of the inhabitants are still in them, hiding in the cellars.

The German airforce hasn't let up for one moment; their bombing and machine-gunning has been murderously methodical.

The Germans have also dropped leaflets in French and in English asking us to surrender and showing a map of Northern

France which outlines their front up to the sea, attempting to prove to us that we are completely surrounded. Some of our men who have picked up these messages laugh at them. They don't understand and refuse to believe that we are cut off from the rest of France. To them it is propaganda which is just as well.

One hour after my arrival, while I am washing up in a pail of cold water, trying to get rid of some of the dust which covers me and which I can even feel between my teeth, terrific explosions shake the buildings and some remaining windowpanes crash around me. I run out in the street to see what is happening. Three miles east of here, the Phalempin woods are erupting in flames and smoke like a volcano. These woods were filled with ammunition dumps belonging mostly to the French Seventh Army. They apparently have been hit and now the thousands of shells which filled them are being transformed into a useless gigantic display of fireworks.

20.00 hrs. The Major and the troops pull up in the courtyard. Although I know that they have gone through much to harass and exhaust them, and that Bruce and Tim have had a terrible day, when I see the look on their faces I know that another tragedy has happened—as if John's death were not enough. The Major's hand grips my arm tensely as he draws me away from the armored cars towards the house. He tells me that brave young Andrew has been killed this afternoon.

I can see plainly how deeply moved the Major is. I ask no questions and make no comment. It is only later on that I find out through the others how gallantly he went to his death while attacking a greatly superior force of enemy tanks. Poor boy!

This puts the squadron's score at three officers killed and four men wounded in less than twenty-four hours. We are all so depressed that we can't even speak to each other and our supper is left untouched. The only thing that seems to help a bit is a little whisky. I feel so badly that I leave the room and walk aimlessly around the courtyard in the dark. As I pass by the window of the room where Tich, Machin and our cook have prepared our supper, I can see the three men sitting mournfully staring into space around a table illuminated by a melting candle which flickers over their untouched food. It is as if the whole squadron were holding a sad vigil tonight communing with the memory of these three gallant men we loved so well.

Returning to the house, I crawl miserably into a corner of the room and lie down on the floor to sleep.

FIFTEENTH DAY

Friday, May 24th

IT SEEMS AS if I have slept only a minute when I am
awakened at 2 A.M. Orders are to pack up and get ready
to move forward immediately in the direction of Lens
and Vimy. We wait for hours, but the order to march never
comes. The situation has deteriorated so much in that sector
that there is probably nothing we can do to help.

At 5.00 hrs. we are ordered northwards to the village of Bois
Grenier, four miles south of Armentieres. We arrive there two
hours later and, though it is filled with Belgian refugees, the
billeting for the now much-reduced squadron is quickly done.
Two farm houses easily take care of the remaining troops, and
a small villa for the officers.

We spend a quiet day in that small village. An amazingly
quiet day. No rumbling of guns reaches us, not a single plane
flies overhead. Birds are singing in the cloudless sky. This
quiet interlude perplexes some of us and even causes rumors that
there has been sort of an armistice. Personally I wonder if it
is not rather the lull before the storm.

Anyway, we all put this day to good use, wash up, do some
laundry work, and I even write a letter which I know will never
reach its destination. Meanwhile, the armored cars are serviced,
the weapons cleaned and the crews get a well-deserved rest.

Before dinner, we gather in a neighboring manure-littered
courtyard around a small portable radio, a gift of Lord Nuffield

to the troops, which was set up on the rear of a lorry, and listen
to His Majesty deliver his Empire Day Message. The men stand
at attention while the weak batteries of the damaged set sputter
forth "God Save the King," and they hear with grave attention
and respect the voice of their ruler, which is barely audible. Then
I notice their chests out-thrust and their eyes gleam with pride
as these last words of their sovereign's speech reach their ears:
". . . Let us go forward to that task as one man, a smile on
our lips, and our heads held high. And with God's help, we
shall not fail."

An inspiring sight, this small group of battle-worn men standing in a rural courtyard at the drawing in of day, so far from their
homeland, and yet suddenly taken there in spirit for a fleeting
moment by the magic of a battered radio haltingly transmitting
to them the voice of their King.

I feel, somehow, as though I had intruded on a family gathering
and that it would be becoming to tiptoe away, if I could, leaving
these Englishmen together.

SIXTEENTH DAY

Saturday, May 25th

REVEILLE AT 6.00 hrs. and we move off towards Belgium at 7.00 A.M. The enemy has broken through the Belgium lines south of Bruges and north of Courtrai. Our regiment's mission is to keep watch on the left flank of the British 2d Corps on the Lys River and gain contact with the right flank of the Belgians.

8.30 hrs. We have just crossed the Belgian border at Le Bizet, north of Armentieres, with orders to reconnoiter east of Roulers within the Belgian sector and make certain of the enemy's positions.

We have forty miles to go and as we speed northwards, we pass over ground hallowed to the British, Hogstreet, Ypres, Paschendaele, finally arriving at Roulers by ten o'clock.

The town is animated; all quite normal. The stores are open and filled with plenty of appetizing merchandize. The people have not fled, nor do they intend to. Bruce's troop leaves us to take up a position somewhere east along the Mandel Canal. While the Major reports to the Colonel, Machin and I decide to spend a few of the belgas which are burning our pockets and stock up with fresh fruit, vegetables, etc.

At one of the shops I buy a large flask of brandy. It might be very useful in case we are captured. I could then get tight and laugh at my captors. And they would want to know why I was laughing and I wouldn't tell them. The Germans wouldn't like it because they always want to know the why of everything.

When I show my prize bottle to Andrew, he asks me to save half of it for him, so we can laugh together. Then he takes me along in the staff car to find the whereabouts of a Belgian infantry brigade which we have been told is holding a line between Ingelmunster and Winkel St. Eloi.

So soon as we get out of the town, we run into intermittent shelling by 105 mm. howitzer H.E.'s. This doesn't stop us and we go through Rumbeke before we halt. Bruce's troop is under heavy artillery fire and has just had a car put out of action. Very heavy stuff is crashing on and around the road, but we make contact with the C.P. of the Belgian Infantry Division and return to Roulers.

A French captain drives up, stops his car and introduces himself. He is the liaison officer of the French Northern Armies group. He has come to get information about the Belgian positions and to find the battle headquarters of the Belgian Army Corps holding this sector. I tell him that it is at Aardappelhoek, one mile east of here. Andrew also gives him what information we have collected about the enemy since this morning.

He tells us that the famous General Giraud, who had just been named to the command of the 9th Army, has been captured by the Germans. This is bad news, indeed. Then, taking me aside, he asks me if I have heard rumors about the British Army pulling out towards the coast. The French Army intends to fight around Lille, Douai, and along the Lys River. It has not lost hope of making a push through the German lines toward the Somme. I tell him that I have heard nothing of such plans, but even if they existed, I would not know because I am too far down the ladder, and that, anyway, the regiment to which I am attached has been too concerned with fighting rear-guard actions to be interested in high strategy. He listens without comment and departs, after shaking hands with me and the Major.

My talk with Captain L. confirms a feeling which I have had for a long time, that there is a definite lack of liaison between the Allied Armies. The French Army long ago had envisaged what might happen in such a case and had inaugurated during this war a new system whereby French liaison officers were assigned to the British fighting forces, not merely as interpreters, as in the last war, but as active parts of combat units. These liaison officers, who had been trained in the use of British weapons, were not to be content to stay with the transport echelons and be used only for feeding and billeting purposes. But in too many instances they were regarded by the British as a nuisance and were sometimes even treated with suspicion. They were often not advised of tactical moves, with the result that there were increasing instances of British guns shooting up French tanks and vice versa. These most regrettable occurrences would certainly have been avoided if all the French liaison officers had been the right men in the right places and put in a position where they could do their job properly. In some regiments, though, such as mine, the Colonel made intelligent use of us, the result being that we always had the closest and friendliest cooperation with the French and Belgian units we were called upon to support.

16.00 hrs. Roulers has had its first air raid and the civil population have run for shelter. The Grande Place is deserted when the Major and I go forward once more to try and effect contract with the Colonel commanding the infantry on the line somewhere west of Izegem. After we pass Rombeke, the cannonade becomes a rolling barrage reminiscent of those I heard in the last war. It is laid down on Winkle St. Eloi by the Belgian artillery in position near Devinke. We are told at the O.P. the Germans are attacking the whole sector at this moment, regardless of cost.

We move on to Okene, a small hamlet where we find the Infantry Colonel's C.P. He tells us that the enemy has succeeded in gaining foothold in Izegem, not quite a mile away, and it seems that the Belgian infantry now holding out at Ingelmunster will have to retreat or they will be cut off.

We return to Roulers at once as the Major wants to report this new development to our Colonel immediately by wireless telephone.

17.00 hrs. The Belgian troops are now withdrawing along the canal towards Roulers and we get orders to proceed five miles west. We start at once.

We are halted in a small hamlet, one mile northeast of West Roozebeke. Heinkels and Messerschmitts have been after us for more than an hour and the attack is still on. The Major and I are crouching behind the wall of a smelly pigsty. I duck each time I hear the bullets punching holes through its tiled roof. Our cars are hidden under sheds around the farmyard. The neighboring fields and hangars of the adjoining granary are filled with troops belonging to a Belgian artillery supply echelon. Their terrified horses are milling around wildly, neighing with fear and running into the barbed wire fences as they try to get away. Every time a bomb crashes, many of them are killed. The personnel, too, seem to be suffering heavy casualties. On the highway directly ahead of us three trucks have been stopped, their drivers killed by the strafing. There is nothing we can do about it, but wait and hope. At first we try shooting at the planes with Bren guns, but give it up as a bad job. The more we shoot at them, the more they come back at us. If we keep quiet, they may forget us.

22.00 hrs. It is dark now and we get orders to drive to Wijtschate, about six miles south of Ypres. The road is blocked by such a quantity of British and French vehicles headed north that it is practically impossible to move. The night is very dark. No one can use headlights and I wonder how the drivers can make any headway at all against this unending stream of trucks, guns, and infantrymen which fills the highway, overflows on the neighboring fields and leaves us no room to pass. It takes us more than two hours to cover twenty miles and when we reach Wijtschate, we have to remain in the cars to wait for further orders.

SEVENTEENTH DAY

NONE OF US has had food or sleep when we pull out of this nightmare at 3.30 A.M., taking a country road to Kemmel. Here, too, we encounter the same traffic jams and it is nearly daybreak when we leave Kemmel for Nieukirk which is our final destination. Gray German transport planes glide ominously overhead, making very little noise and barely clearing the hilltops.

The squadron draws up on the square in front of the church at Nieukirk. Men and officers alike are close to exhaustion from lack of food and sleep. Our transport echelon arrived here last night, but it is billeted in a group of farmhouses a mile southwest of the village, too far to be of any help.

The church door is wide open, and from where I stand I can see the altar brightly lit with candles and the priest standing in his white and gold vestments giving communion.

Seeking solace, I step into this unbelievable haven of peace, of "peace on earth, good will toward men" and kneel down. The sight of the ancient walls surrounding these rituals which have gone on unchanged for centuries through the upheavals of war and shocks of revolution suddenly restores some faith in myself and in humanity, a faith of which at the moment I am in dire need. When I leave the church I feel mentally more serene, on solider spiritual ground.

Andrew tells me that he thinks I can do with a little rest

and, as he won't need me, he wants me to remain here this morning. I am to keep the staff car and he will send for me if necessary. He is going off now with the armored cars to Ypres. I am so sleepy and spent that I am more than grateful for his kind thought. Machin and I find a small house on the main street where the good-hearted owner lets us have two mattresses to lie on.

8.00 hrs. Shattered glass from the windowpanes flying around and terrific explosions wake me. The house rocks and, as I stumble to the door, it seems as if the ground is rising under my feet. Everything in the room crashes to the floor. Barefooted and in my underwear, leaping over glass splinters, I erupt into the street.

Bombs are falling all around, shaking the very foundations of the village. The Luftwaffe is apparently set on destroying it. More than twelve planes roar over the main street dropping tons of explosives. The place is an inferno of smoke and fire, falling bricks. Geysers of earth and tongues of flame leap into the sky. For three minutes or more, that seem endless, I cower under a wall holding my breath, my legs shaking, while houses to the right and left are smashed to the ground. Two hundred yards up the road a convoy of more than twenty ammunition trucks is hit repeatedly and blows up with deafening explosions. Shells and men's bodies fly through the air. The ammunition cases keep on exploding an hour after the planes disappear, making it impossible for anyone to rescue the wounded.

So soon as we can, Machin and I run back to our room, hurry into our clothes and, dashing across the street, make for the place where we have hidden the staff car. By some miracle it is undamaged. We jump into it and drive to the farm where our transport echelon is billeted. The narrow road leading up the hill is pitted with huge craters, beside which lay many dead and wounded.

I find our transport echelon saddened by the death of Lance-Corporal Chandler who has just been killed. He is their only casualty. His comrades bury him on a hillock just outside the farm under some shady trees. Later the men tell me that about the farm most of the bombs dropped in the fields around the buildings and they show me the carcasses of ten cows, victims of the raid.

11.00 hrs. More planes come over, but this time two of them are shot down by antiaircraft fire; others are after Bailleul and Armentieres. During the whole morning, there has been loud and incessant thundering of artillery fire toward the east in the direction of Warneton and Ypres.

A heavy cloudburst gives us a respite from the raiders. This is the first rain we have had since the offensive started sixteen days ago. I take shelter in a small shack where I find an old man sitting quietly smoking his clay pipe as if nothing disturbing were going on around him. We get to talking and I discover that he earns his living in rather an extraordinary way. Since the last war, in which he took part, he has been smuggling coarse tobacco over the French border two miles away and selling scrap iron which he dug out of the surrounding battlefields—rusty remains of the millions of shells which plowed up this sector. This in a modest manner, of course, just enough to keep him provided with food, shelter, tobacco and an occasional nip of schnapps. He tells me that the only thing worrying him about this present war is that he thinks the indiscriminate way in which bombs are dropping all over the countryside will make it more difficult to collect later. He also fears that perhaps the German steel won't be quite up to quality! He then confides to me that his business, which was beginning to wane, underwent a boom when this war started and the price of scrap metal doubled.

After the cloudburst I leave this strange old man, wishing him health and a good crop, and, as I walk down the road and turn around to give one more look at the shack, I see him standing on the doorstep rubbing his hands and looking hopefully up at the sky.

14.00 hrs. I receive orders from the Major to proceed at once to Woesten, five miles northwest of Ypres, but I am told to avoid the Ypres road which is filled with civilians fleeing the city, and also from Poperingen, as the French D.L.M. transports are moving through that sector and it is a constant target for the bombers. I decide to go through Valmertinge and Elverdinge.

After I have spent two hours trying to find billets in Woesten, our armored cars arrive and Andrew tells me we are going on to Westvleteren, five miles northwest, a village near the Furnes highway. I scramble on to the back of Bruce's armored car and we speed on. He tells me that the Germans have breached the line between Menin and Warneton and are driving a wedge between the Belgian and British troops in the direction of Wijtschate.

20.00 hrs. I have been trying desperately to find shelter in this village for our cars and the troops, but it is already filled with soldiers of all nationalities and refugees. I finally get the transport echelon, the armored cars and their crews some space in a farm just outside the village, near the crossroad to Poperingen. It is far from being an ideal billet as there is constant traffic going by.

An hour later, after having walked at least three miles and been turned down by every houseowner, I lose patience and drag the burgomaster from his dinner to force the unwilling female owner of a small house to accept our mess.

"You must sleep on the brick floor and be careful to leave the place clean," says the vinegary spinster, but Machin and Tich have already occupied a corner of her stove and they tell me that if I can keep this witch out of the kitchen they may be able to give us a hot meal. Bruce and Tim have fallen asleep the minute they sat down on the floor, their heads lopped on their chests.

The Major says that it looks as if we might get a few hours' sleep and not leave until daylight tomorrow.

EIGHTEENTH DAY

Monday, May 27th.

WE ARE ALL packed up and ready to go at 5.00, awaiting further orders. They come at 6.00. We are to stay here probably all day and rest. This is welcome news as our cars need plenty of servicing.

The morning drags on with the men sleeping, washing, and cleaning weapons, hardly disturbed by the enemy aircraft of all descriptions, but mostly bombers, which are actively plastering the roads around us.

Poperingen, five miles south, has been a constant target. The northern part of our village has been bombed, too, but there are antiaircraft batteries around which keep the Jerries at an altitude where their aim is not very accurate. The closest they have got to our farm so far is two hundred yards west, where they have done a pretty good job at digging up a meadow.

Our Colonel comes to visit us at noon and we learn the seriousness of the situation. There is no further question of trying to make a break for it through the ever-thickening German lines to join up with the French armies in the south. The British High Command has decided that the only way out of the trap is to head for the coast around Dunkirk and get off as many men as possible while other troops try to hold the enemy; these rearguards will be sacrificed, of course. The first to embark will be the wounded, the non-combatants and the numerous troops of the Army Supply Corps. But other troops are getting off, too, and I hear that the tank brigade which made the raid around Arras on May 21st is already safely back in England. I wonder what will happen to us, who have been acting as rearguard ever since May 12th!

There is also bad news from the Belgian side—talk of surrender. If that happens, our left flank will be completely unprotected and we must shorten our line by withdrawing behind the canals running from Nieuport to the region south of Dunkirk. Ypres is still in British hands, but for how long? Roulers has fallen and there seems to be little cohesion in the Belgian lines. German patrols have been encountered many miles this side of them, and wiped out, one in particular as it was trying to get across the Yser-Ypres canal six miles east of here. The French troops, under Generals Blanchard and Prioux, are still holding out around Douai and the Lys River, keeping the Germans at bay along the Franco-Belgian border.

15.00 hrs. Our gracious hostess has locked us out and we have had to settle in a tool shed belonging to the farm where our troops are billeted. We are to stay here tonight and will probably have to sleep in the shed.

The sound of increased firing reaches us now from the east and southeast. More and more German bombers fly over us unchecked.

There was a lull about an hour ago during which three British Hurricanes streaked overhead. It was a most rare and welcome sight, and the troops cheered them as the pilots flapped the wings of the planes and showed their markings.

NINETEENTH DAY

Tuesday, May 28th.

RAIN IS FALLING when we awake at 6.00 after a good night's sleep on the damp brick floor. Though my ribs ache a little, I feel relaxed from the rest—but not for long!
I hear that what was only a rumor yesterday is official news today. The King of the Belgians has capitulated in the field, surrendering himself and his army to the German commanders, just as Napoleon III did to Bismarck at Sedan in 1870. The order to the Belgian Army to cease firing was issued at 4.00 this morning, two hours ago. Our left flank is wide open! Yypres and Kemmel are now in German hands. For a few seconds, as I realize the far-reaching consequences of this, I feel as if I had been punched in the stomach. I think we all do. It is a terrific blow.

10.00 hrs. As a result of the Belgian surrender, our squadron is ordered to proceed immediately to the north to patrol the Loo Canal between Alveringen and Furnes. This means that we, at least for awhile, are not heading for Dunkirk.

I am totally unprepared for the sight that greets us as we reach the Furnes highway. It recalls the paintings of Napoleon's retreat from Russia. Brand new trucks, tractors, guns of every calibre, line the ditches and fields. Millions of dollars worth of entirely new British equipment lies in the mud, abandoned by the troops who have already left the battle and are on their way to embarkation. It is a horrible and disheartening sight. Most of this equipment looks as if it has never been used. When we see the scores of cannon in the ditches by the roadside we can't help wondering why it has not been brought into the Dunkirk perimeter to be used for its defense.

We turn right at the Winken crossroad and reach Oeren, a mile and a half north of Alveringen by 10.00 o'clock. Our mission is to patrol the area beyond the canal which we are glad to hear is held by the Dragoons of the French D.L.M. The soldiers of these hard-fighting cavalry divisions have long since won the admiration and respect of every man in our squadron, whose faces always brighten when they know they are fighting with the D.L.M.'s at our side.

Squadron H.Q. is established in a quaint little farmhouse surrounded by a moat. The whole countryside looks like Holland, but the tulips are missing. It is raining hard and the road surfaces are fast turning into mud. As I stand on the small bridge over the moat, I can count more than sixty German light bombers cruising below the clouds at less than 500 feet.

14.00 hrs. The downpour continues. Thousands of Belgian soldiers pass us on their way to Nieuport to give themselves up. It is an overwhelmingly mournful sight. I talk to some of them who feel they should have gone on fighting. But they all say that, after all, their King knows best and, if he has ordered them to surrender, it is probably because there was nothing else to do. Others seem happy that they are going home and good-naturedly gibe at us.

Meanwhile the Major has pushed boldly on to Nieuport and had a lively encounter with a motorized detachment which was about to cross over the bridge. A little farther on two troops of the regiment who had pushed forward with great daring across the canal have attacked and thrown back some enemy units who were trying to sneak over this unprotected area. Many Germans were killed during this action, and had our troops not been there at the time, the enemy would certainly have got across our perimeter and, infiltrating along the coast, might have cut us off completely.

18.00 hrs. Our orders are to withdraw behind the canal as the bridge at Alveringen is blown up. Then we proceed to Oeren where our supply echelon is waiting for us.

There are only five armored cars left in the squadron now. In a few hours they will go forth again to support the French Dragoons holding the bridge at Furnes. German patrols which were observed going through Dixmude at 18.00 hrs. are already approaching the canal a few hundred yards away and we can hear intense machine-gunning and artillery fire all along the front. The gun fire is especially sharp and spectacular. Some batteries are very near and their shells swish by over our heads unceasingly, on their way to blast the enemy's concentrations.

23.00 hrs. We have just had something to eat and we have been greatly heartened after a talk with our Colonel, who is as cool and keen as ever. His untiring courage and intelligent leadership of the regiment have just been rewarded by a D.S.O., which is a great compliment and joy to all of us.

TWENTIETH DAY

Wednesday, May 29th.

IT IS 1.00 A.M. and we are still sitting with the Colonel. Bruce and Tim are sitting up, too, but they are fast asleep. The Major, wide awake and rarin' to go, is planning for a heroic last stand at a certain bridge. To make up for our deficiency in armored cars, he wants to use a forlorn-hope party of men on foot. The cooks, Machin and Tich, volunteer with the rest for the job and, though I inwardly question the soundness of the move as good military strategy, I half-heartedly offer my services on condition that I am allowed to have a sleep beforehand. If I am not, I certainly wouldn't be able, in my present state, to draw a bead on an elephant at a hundred paces. That would require keeping my eyes open and that is the one thing of which I feel totally incapable.

I unclose my eyes fifteen minutes later. The Colonel is gone, the whisky bottle is empty, and the candle is guttering. I crawl to a corner of a room and, curling upon the wooden floor, lay my head on my gas respirator and go back to sleep.

Two hours later we are up, again packed and ready to obey any orders.

4.00 hrs. Our five armored cars and the fighting lorry rumble slowly out of the farm through the gluey mud in the cold drizzly night. We are heading north on highway 65, towards Furnes and Nieuport. The transport echelon will leave at 5.00 hrs. for Ghyveldes, a village six miles northeast of Dunkirk.

The farther we go the more the roads and the adjacent fields have taken on the aspect of dumps filled with what once was the fine materiel of the B.E.F. Overturned trucks, equipment, broken cases with thousands of unopened cans spilled out, heaps of cigarette packages and clothing are strewn everywhere in the mire. As the day lightens, we can see many freshly-dug graves and bloated horses putrifying in the fields. Long lines of worn-out troops trudge wearily on amidst the wreckage. Troops of every description, French, British, Belgian, all in disorder, all retreating.

5.00 hrs. The squadron's cars have taken positions back of the bridges at Nieuport. We find the French Dragoons already established there and in control of the situation. The enemy has not shown up since their setback yesterday, but German field guns are getting the range of the bridges and several 105-mm shells burst above them. A Henschel observation plane hovers overhead, an ominous token of unpleasant things to come.

14.00 hrs. My lunch biscuit has been ruined by an extremely and disagreeably intrusive dive-bomber attack which lasted a full half hour. The Dragoons have suffered many casualties as the Stukas took turns diving down at us with sirens screaming while their light bombs exploded with terrific claps on the stone-paved streets. All the bridges on the canal are being blown up. The Belgians who haven't already crossed will have to remain on our side.

15.00 hrs. The forward troops receive orders to withdraw and join the regimental rendezvous at Gyveldes. The French have flooded the whole district south of Furnes as a defense against enemy tanks, and the narrow roads, which are barely above the level of water-covered fields, are so jammed with retreating troops that we proceed only with the greatest difficulty. Highway 65, which we have to follow for a while, is shelled intermittently by 105-mm H.E. They appear to come from the direction of Poperingen, southeast of us. We finally reach the French border and halt south of Gyveldes.

The moment which we have all dreaded has finally arrived. The battle-scarred armored care are lined up alongside the canal.

The Major gives the order to dismount. He directs that all cars be stripped of weapons, ammunition, and any other equipment which can be of use. This done, a final order comes from him. Their motors roaring for the last time, the cars are backed into the canal and blown up.

Heavily-laden, we move toward Ghyveldes, trudging slowly under our burdens. Many a head turns back to give a farewell look at the armored cars, our faithful companions which, though inadequate in many ways, have rendered unfailing service in most difficult conditions. Now merely hulks of steel, they sluggishly sink into their muddy graves.

We are all gathered in a large field on the outskirts of Ghyveldes. Officers and men alike are destroying and burning their personal kit, everything they will not be able to carry along with them. A huge bonfire has been started. Suitcases full of linen, boots, records, etc., everything we have carried with us so long and which we cherish, are reluctantly thrown into the blaze.

The sky is mantled with black smoke from the blazing city of Dunkirk. Under that sable roof, suddenly six British fighter planes flash over us and vanish toward the Channel. They are followed by a flight of enemy bombers heading for Dunkirk. The tremendous roar of all those motors mingles with the steady rumble of artillery fire from the southeast.

20.00 hrs. We are under strong and savage air attack. Squadrons of Heinkels and Messerschmitts are machine-gunning and bombing the village with all they've got. Dozens of abandoned French artillery horses that were grazing in our field have been killed; the others are whinnying and galloping around us, trying to escape. The din is terrific. Every available weapon has been turned against the planes and thousands of bullets are whizzing in every direction. I have taken refuge in a shallow ditch. To quiet my nerves more than anything else, I, too, am shooting at them with a borrowed rifle. I crouch low, for the danger from the ground-fire is as great as that from the air.

21.00 hrs. The noise has subsided. We stand around, not knowing what to do and wait for orders. Andrew has captured one of the French artillery horses and riding bareback gone off to the village to find out what he can. Three miles back of us the French cavalry have moved up to their defensive positions back of the Colme Canal and their game 75-mm guns are already barking defiance at the oncoming enemy.

Our Colonel arrives. We hear that we must be ready to leave for the coast at 3.00 A.M. Many ships have been sunk by the German airforce this afternoon and evening, so the evacuation is not proceeding very fast. But it appears that we have been promised air protection for tomorrow. I feel very miserable as I think of the thousands of French soldiers of the Cavalry Corps trapped and cut off from us sixty miles away, fighting to the last around Douai and Lille. It is their sacrifice which may perhaps enable us to get away. Machin brings me a cup of hot tea to cheer me up. I roll up in a blanket, lie down on the wet grass near an abandoned truck and try to sleep, and not think of tomorrow.

TWENTY-FIRST DAY

Thursday, May 30th

IT IS HARDLY past three in the morning when we assemble in the dark and move off toward Adinkerke, carrying on our shoulders Bren guns, heavy Boys antitank rifles and cases filled with ammunition. At first we follow a smuggler's path along a ridge of sand dunes lying a mile south of the main Dunkirk-Furnes highway. It is heavy going and we often have to stop to allow the more tired ones to catch up. After about two miles, through this winding path, we cross the French border and, turning north into Belgium once more, reach the highway which runs alongside the Dunkirk-Furnes Canal. Here we halt again and sit for awhile in the bordering ditch to catch our breath. Two more miles, that seem like ten, bring us to Adinkerque. We halt back of a farm near a narrow bridge over the canal.

I am worn out and soaked with sweat, and for me it is high time we stopped. I feel as though I can't walk a step further. There is an old-fashioned well in the courtyard with plenty of clear water, so, while the cooks make tea, I draw a pailfull and, kneeling by it, soak my head with relief in its welcome coolness.

The Colonel drives up, assembles the officers and tells us that from the look of things we may get off, but warns that if we are to get aboard a ship we most probably shall have to swim for it. He advises us to get rid of everything we have except weapons, ammunition and our respirators.

Some of the men have found a dozen abandoned bicycles,

153

probably left there by the Belgian troops. They will make mar-
velous carriers for the heavier guns and our ammunition cases
when we move.

11.00 hrs. We are assembled on the side of the road waiting
for the order to march across the bridge leading to La Panne,
in happier days a summer resort on the coast. After waiting for
a half hour, the signal to march is given and we start off toward
the canal in troop column formation with wide intervals between
each troop. A platoon of British infantry guards the bridge and
British officers stop the French soldiers who want to go toward
the coast. Only British soldiers are allowed to cross this bridge
and it is only after my Major and Bruce, linking their arms
through mine, insist that I am part of the regiment and that
wherever they go, I shall go, too, that I am allowed to keep on
with my squadron.

I am suprised at this, and when I see Captain Ciriez, French
liaison officer with this British Army Corps, who is standing at
the far side of the bridge, I tell him so. His job is to detour the
French troops towards the south to Bray-Dunes and Malo les
Bains, the only points where the French will be taken off. This,
he says, is to avoid confusion as strict discipline and control is
needed in an operation of this kind.

After crossing the bridge, there is a good two-mile walk before
reaching La Panne which we can see, and hear, is being blasted
by artillery fire as well as bombed from the air. The road runs
through the dunes under clumps of pine trees. It is jammed
with abandoned trucks which are being emptied little by little
of their contents by hundreds of stragglers in French uniform
who are camping gypsy-fashion around fires in the neighboring
dunes. Some of them are drunk.

This lack of discipline among my own countrymen which is
being displayed in front of British soldiers, who I know have
always had the greatest respect for the French Army, infuriates
me. I stop a group of men and try to shame them into an appre-
ciation of their behavior. After hearing only a few sentences
of what they have to say, it is I who grow embarrassingly uncomfortable.

These soldiers are all men belonging to the older reserves. The gist of their replies is that they know they are going to be left behind. They have been told that the authorities have decided to give first chance for escape to the younger fighting men who will be able to get right back into the scrap. So they, the older men of the Services of Supply, have to stay behind and take what comes.

It is difficult to argue with these men, who are now sitting around in the sand looking at me defiantly and consoling themselves by eating and drinking everything those who are leaving them have abandoned. It would be, I suppose, equally as difficult to argue about life with a man who is dying of a fatal malady and who has only a few hours left. These men, too, have only a few more hours of freedom remaining.

Apologetically, I take leave of them, not daring to look back and face their envious and anxious eyes as they watch us march down the road toward what they regard as safety.

We halt under some pine trees just outside La Panne while our Major goes for orders. The two other squadrons are already here sitting in the shade of the trees and for the first time in a month, I see my friend, Guy, French liaison officer with Squadron B. We have plenty to talk about and Pierre, our colleague from C Squadron, whom I have not seen since Neuville-St. Vaast joins us. We forget the bombardment as we chat about the not-so-very agreeable present and try to forecast what the immediate future holds for us.

14.00 hrs. We march off again, go through the town. As we reach the end of a narrow street we smell the tang of a salty breeze and a few minutes later, beyond a narrow stretch of yellow sand, our eyes behold the glorious sight of the splashing surf and beyond, stretching to the end of the horizon, the dark green waves over which we may be borne to England.

We establish ourselves in two deserted villas on the sea-front. Then we hear that for us, at least, there is no immediate prospect of embarkation, for our squadron is assigned to police duty on the beach, to see that what embarkations are made are accomplished in good order. Four Bofors antiaircraft guns are on the sands opposite our squadron headquarters. A little farther down large tarpaulins have been spread over the sand, and trucks have been driven over them at low tide down to the sea, forming a kind of jetty at high water.

The sun is very hot, the sea calm and inviting. Thousands of British soldiers line the waterfront, patiently waiting for a boat; but no boats seem to be coming near the shore. These men have been here all day and not one yet has been embarked. Grim-looking, but hopeful, they stand, seemingly unmindful of the German shells which are plopping into the waves and splashing up geysers of water where these long-awaited boats should be.

The German battery that is firing at the beach is not very far away, perhaps four miles east beyond Koksyde.

15.00 hrs. I have wandered all through the town in search of food for the squadron and been partially successful. Every house is overflowing with refugees who, having after superhuman effort reached the western shore of their country, now find themselves hopelessly trapped.

When I return to the waterfront with Trooper Machin and Lance Corporal Aldrich, laden with supplies, I see that two destroyers have moved close into shore and are now taking on men. They keep changing position all the time to avoid the shells that are still splashing around them. After awhile, as the fire increases in intensity, all embarkation is stopped and they steam off slowly towards Dunkirk.

The enemy guns shorten their range and high explosive shells start to fall higher up on the beach and on the boardwalk near us. There is no cover, so we crouch where we are and wait.

Two hours have gone by. Several destroyers and a light cruiser now are standing about two miles off shore and engaging the German batteries which are shelling us. First we see bright orange flashes spurt from their guns; then we hear the thunder of their broadside hurling tons of explosives over our heads toward the German lines near Furnes, four miles southeast of here. It is a magnificent spectacle, and we have ring-side seats. The immense black clouds of smoke stretching for miles out to sea billow over

Dunkirk, getting thicker and rising ever higher in the sky. The oil reserves must be on fire.

The roar of engines fills the air. A huge formation of heavy German bombers flies straight at us, at less than a thousand feet. The crews of the Boförs battery have seen them and the four guns open up at full speed. Tracer shells streak through the air which is rapidly filled with black smoke and the dark smudges of shell bursts. Bren guns are shouldered and add their sharp crackle to the ear-rending racket. Unperturbed, in perfect formation, the bombers fly over us, dropping their bombs as they pass. The anti-aircraft fire increases in intensity as French heavy machine guns in the dunes blaze away at them. Yet they keep coming! There must be more than a hundred of them.

I can see antiaircraft shells pumping straight into one of the black bombers. Its left wing is on fire, but it keeps in formation and drops its bomb. Then it swings seaward, becomes a flaming torch, and plunges into the waves with a huge splash a few hundred yards off shore. Another is hit. And another. They, too, crash into the sea, exploding as they hit the water. The antiaircraft crews are working like demons, swinging their guns around and changing red-hot barrels every minute. But the bombers keep on coming. The noise and the commotion are so great that I feel my legs shaking under me and my heart pounding in my chest. Yet the excitement is so intense that there is no place for fear.

I am standing flat against the wall of a villa. Two British soldiers of another regiment are crouching by my side. One of them seems near the breaking point. He keeps a handkerchief stuffed in his mouth so as not to scream. His face is the color of clay and his dilated eyes alone show what he is undergoing in nervous tension. I offer him brandy, but he shakes his head in refusal.

The air is thick with the reek and smell of smoke and explosives, but the roar of the motors is fading. The last bomber finally has flown over, heading up the beach toward the north. The guns have stopped firing. All is calm once more, until, coming from the sea, six more planes soar out of the smoke like gray flashes.

Hell is let loose again as every weapon goes into action. But, as they pass overhead, we see in a flash the circles of the R.A.F. under their wings. Everyone yells, "Cease firing," and the firing stops after a few seconds. Luckily no one has been hit.

Offshore, I see the signal lamp of one of the warships blinking towards us. One of the men next to me, who is a signaller, takes down the message. It says: "The aircraft which you have so enthusiastically received are friendly." Whoever sent this message certainly had a sense of humor, but I am afraid not much sense of brevity or speed.

19.00 hrs. Two of the destroyers have moved in towards shore, and embarkation has been resumed. The Major comes up from the water line where he has been waiting ankle-deep in water helping soldiers into longboats. While he drinks a cup of hot tea and eats a sandwich, we talk of our chances of getting to England. He thinks they are slim. But I think differently. I feel sure that the High Command will do everything it can to save a man of such military calibre as our Colonel. They will need him later and I know that he will not leave the beach until the last man of his regiment is safely on board.

Andrew and Bruce are to be on duty all night and when I ask the Major if there is anything I can do to help, he tells me there is nothing he can think of except to keep smiling—if I can.

TWENTY-SECOND DAY

Friday, May 31st.

SHELLS OF 105-mm crashing in the streets and through the rooftops around our villa wake me abruptly after a good sleep on the wooden floor. I find Andrew in the front room, worn out from his all-night vigil over the embarkation and from standing so long in the cold water. His expression is grim, smileless. We sit down to a light breakfast to the accompaniment of the howling and banging of exploding shells. As it seems that we have yet no prospect of getting off, he asks me to go out again into the town and see what I can find in the way of food. We empty all our pockets of what money we have left and I take it along for a buying spree.

Dodging shrapnel and running from house to house with Machin in tow, I find an open bakery where I buy several loaves of bread. Then we have to climb over a back wall into a grocery store where we succeed in getting some sardines and cheese, paying for them with almost their weight in gold. What is left of the money, we invest in wine and beer and though exploding shells force us to drop flat on the ground many times on our way back, we manage to return to the squadron with our precious cargo unharmed. We are welcomed like long-lost brothers.

12.00 hrs. The destroyers that have been lying offshore and taking off men all morning have pulled out again because of intense shelling from German batteries. We are receiving heavier stuff now, 155-mm at least, and the fire is getting too accurate

159

for safety. Each time the destroyers put to sea, gloom settles along the beach and everyone wears a long face. To add to our worries, the antiaircraft battery has been withdrawn during the night and we are now left without protection in case of a new bombing attack.

13.00 hrs. More and more 155-mm H.E.'s are dropping on the town, tearing up the streets and smashing the pretty villas along the boardwalk. But now we don't mind, for the squadron has been relieved of police duty and it looks as if we might get off after all. There are no boats offshore, but the morale of the squadron is good. Everyone is optimistic.

An hour later, the Major arrives with the news that the whole regiment is to assemble on the beach below the dunes at the western end of the town. We leave the boardwalk without regrets and march off single file in the heavy sand towards the rendezvous.

We find the other squadrons waiting there and for the first time since May 10th, all the Lancers are reunited. The men are lying around in the hot sun waiting for the return of the Colonel who has gone off toward Dunkirk. Andrew and Bruce have found some deck chairs in which they lie sunbathing as if it were just an ordinary summer day. I am about to imitate them and stretch out in the warm sand when the noise of aircraft motors makes me sit up and take notice. A flight of German light bombers is coming down the beach.

Fifteen seconds later, bombs come screaming towards us thundering down on the dunes, the shore, and on the hotel that stands at the western tip of the town a few hundred yards away. The Commander-in-Chief of the B.E.F., General Lord Gort, was resting in this same hotel only a few hours ago. The hotel is hit repeatedly. I dig into the sand as fast as I can. I can't help remembering childhood days when I used to dig similar holes on beaches with a little wooden shovel. My friend, Guy, has found a small plank and we soon have a hole deep enough to enable us both to crawl in. While we are thus engaged, the planes fly two miles out to sea and attack a destroyer which shoots one of them down. Then, thinking we are an easier target, they make a wide turn, come back, dive low to machine-gun us, rise again, drop five more bombs and, following the beach, disappear toward the smoke cloud which covers the whole of the Dunkirk area.

15.00 hrs. Our Colonel arrives in a small car which his driver has found on the beach. The heavier weapons are placed in it and we are ordered to march towards Dunkirk, ten miles away. The Major places the squadron in arrow formation and we start off, plodding slowly through the heavy sands.

We have been marching for about an hour under the blazing sun and our formation has drawn out somewhat as we have been machine-gunned and bombed three times. Several of our men have been wounded.

The Major walks ahead unflinchingly. He is shouldering parts of the kits of many exhausted men and has not once slackened his pace or ducked to dodge bombs and bullets. His magnificent bravery gives us courage to keep on going.

The beach is littered with ships that have run ashore. Huge, sleek-looking unexploded German torpedos lie glistening at the edge of the waves. A fairly large steamer has been completely cut in two by a bomb and is stuck in the sand. Dead bodies line the shore. Other corpses bob up and down in the surf and are swept in by the waves. The dunes to our left are filled with French soldiers whose machine guns vainly try to keep the German planes away.

19.00 hrs. We are still stumbling along, dodging bombs, and have just passed the sanitorium of Braydunes. We are in France again and have marched over seven miles since leaving La Panne. It has been tough going every inch of the way. Not far ahead I can see the large hotel of Malo Terminus two miles east of Dunkirk. The Colonel's car passes and halts a half mile ahead of us. When we reach him he tells us that we have now come to the end of the road and must take to water. We are going to embark!

Near where we halt, there is a small steamer grounded about a hundred feet offshore, filled with French soldiers. It is waiting for the tide, a constant target for the Heinkels flying above. About a mile out to sea, two boats are slowly moving in our direction. The first is a small excursion steamer, the other a queer-

looking craft—a sand-dredger. Long boats and launches are also
coming toward us and the sailors signal us to come out as far as
we can into the water. The wind is rising and there is quite a
swell as everyone wades out into the cold sea. We are soon
shoulder-deep.

R.A.F. fighters have engaged the Heinkels and dispersed them.
I am too busy keeping my head above the surf to enjoy the
dog-fights, but I do see two enemy bombers hit the waves and
blow up, and a Hurricane dive straight into the sea a few hundred
yards away.

A half hour later all the men have clambered into the
launches and one by one they board the steamer, which pulls out
rapidly as soon as it is full. The only ones left now neck-deep
in the icy water are the Colonel, the three squadron leaders, two
French liaison officers and myself, plus a handful of men. We
are to try and climb onto the dredge which is coming slowly in
toward us.

A heavy swell which washes over my head makes me lose the
haversack I was holding above the water. In this I had put a dry
shirt, a sweater, some few valued personal belongings and my
gas mask. I try in vain to recover it, but it sinks to the bottom
like a stone, waterlogged.

A launch floats near me, but its sides are so high that, try as
I may, I have not the strength to pull myself up, weighted down
by my soaked uniform, my steel helmet and my heavy riding
boots. After several attempts, I am about to give up, loosen my
grip. My fingers are numb. I am sure I cannot hold on another
minute. Then four strong arms hoist me over the side. I fall
like a clod into the bottom of the launch. My aching body feels
dead. All I can hear is the roaring of the German motors sweeping
over us, the screaming of the bombs and the loud explosions which
jar my ears and practically blow the breath out of me. I hear
Pierre, who is sitting next to me, say that a drink of brandy
would be in order. I point to my left pocket and he pulls out my
flask. We pour brandy down our throats as if it were water.

21.00 hrs. I am sitting stark naked on a heap of coal in the
engine room of the dredger. My clothes are hanging near the

furnace to dry, and I am trying to get warm. My whole body is shaking. I don't want to move, but just sit here where it is hot and stare at the flames of the boiler with my mind a complete blank. The craft is crawling along slowly, because a near-hit bomb loosened some bow plates. The stoker says we are averaging only about two knots.

TWENTY-THIRD DAY

Saturday, June 1st

THE CHUG-CHUGGING OF the engine has stopped, and I open my eyes. The stoker tells me we are off our course and lost in a mine-field; we are going to wait for daylight and hope for the best. My clothes are dry and, after making myself as respectable in appearance as means permit, I climb up the iron ladder and join the others who are lying in a huddle inside the wheelhouse. I squeeze between them and go back to sleep with my head to the binnacle and my dirty boots practically on the face of a major.

6.00 hrs. A new day has begun. I am standing on the small deck. All around me men in French and British uniforms are huddled together, lying on the filthy boards, dead to the world, down and out. The skipper has hailed a passing mine-sweeper and has been given his course through a megaphone, so we are on our way again.

I lean over the rail to watch the widening wake, feeling low and very weary. I have lost my personal kit and all that is left now are the bedraggled clothes on my body, some papers, and this diary which I had kept in my pocket. Even my revolver dropped out of its holster when I was being pulled aboard and fell in the water.

I can't yet fully understand what has happened or how it happened during these twenty-one mad days. I feel as if I were emerging from a hell-roaring binge. It dawns upon me with a

165

rush, and for the first time, that the dead we have left behind are really dead—gone!

Seagulls are screaming overhead, land is near. I turn my head into the morning breeze to face the towering cliffs of England, tough bastions of the British Empire which is waiting to welcome us. Soon my friends and I will be back in the fight again. Next time we shall do better.

We have lost the first round, true. But we have gained much in experience. I feel that there will be many more rounds . . . many, many more!

Editor's Note: In all, 211,532 fit men and 13,053 casualties, of the British Army, and 112,526 Allied troops were embarked at Dunkirk and beaches. Most of them under conditions akin to those described by Henry de la Falaise. The remainder of the French *"Armée du Nord,"* the more than 110,000 men who stayed behind to hold the last defences and thus enable their comrades to embark, were either mowed down when the Germans arrived or are to this day leading miserable lives in the prison camps of Germany.